BURGUNDY
gastronomique

BURGUNDY
gastronomique

OLIVIA CALLEA

FOREWORD BY ANNE WILLAN

PHOTOGRAPHY BY HAMISH PARK

SERIES EDITOR: MARIE-PIERRE MOINE

Conran Octopus

First published in Great Britain in 1995 by
Conran Octopus Limited
37 Shelton Street
London WC2H 9HN

British Library Cataloguing-in-Publication Data
A catalogue record for this book is available from
the British Library.

ISBN 1 85029 710 X

Project Editor **CHARLOTTE COLEMAN-SMITH**
Commissioning Editor **SARAH PEARCE**
Art Editor **KAREN BOWEN**
Text Editor **WENDY DALLAS**
Recipe Editor **BEVERLY LE BLANC**
Home Economist **MEG JANSZ**
Production **JILL MACEY**
Typesetting **LIZA BRUML**

Printed in Hong Kong

NOTE ON RECIPES Both metric and imperial quantities
are given. Use either all metric or all imperial, as
the two are not interchangeable.

CONTENTS

FOREWORD

What a pleasure to learn more about one's home ground! For more than half the year I live in Burgundy, and Olivia Callea paints an evocative picture of this rich, pastoral province which is less than two hours from Paris. She describes not just the countryside and the people, but also the history and the many splendid buildings which date back to the fourteenth-century dukedom, the Burgundian golden age.

Most vividly of all, Olivia Callea recreates the local cooking: *gougères* served with a glass of chilled Chablis; plump duck breasts in a tart fruit sauce; goose stuffed with apples (shades of my Yorkshire childhood!); and a notable cherry cake called *tartouillat*. She talks of asparagus and cherries, of Soumantrain cheese, and of ratafia, the local aperitif. Even truffles are explored, for a type, admittedly inferior to the jet-black diamonds of Périgord, do grow in the sprawling forests of northern Burgundy, named after its main river, the Yonne.

This is just the start of Olivia Callea's tour. She moves south into the Morvan, rural and astonishingly remote from the nearby autoroute. By contrast, to the south-east lies the legendary Côte d'Or, the most valuable stretch of vineyard in the world, then the fertile Charolais, home of renowned beef cattle, and Bresse with its pure-bred chickens.

To pin down the wealth and variety of Burgundian cooking is a tough call, and Olivia Callea succeeds because she describes not just the food, but the people who create and enjoy it. You will meet idealists such as Gérard Maternaud, grower of organic vegetables and herbs, and great chefs such as Marc Meneau with his restaurant l'Espérance, near the basilica of Vézelay. Come and talk to crayfish catchers, stag hunters, jam makers, liqueur distillers and bakers of spice bread who jealously guard their secret recipe.

This is a book to appreciate with a glass of wine, to skim the surface, then to delve into and embark on a serious journey, whether real or imaginary, of this most tempting province of France. Looking at the lush, generous photography, I can hardly wait to start.

FAR LEFT Cattle breeding and milk
production are important agricultural activities
in the lush pastures of Burgundy.
LEFT A member of the Confrérie des Vignerons de
Saint-Vincent de Bourgogne et Mâcon, taking
part in a colourful parade prior to
a celebratory banquet.
RIGHT Wild mushrooms abound
in the forests of Burgundy, particularly
in the Morvan.

ABOVE Bottles of oil awaiting delivery at the
Leblanc warehouse in Iguerande.
RIGHT The simple austerity of the Romanesque
cloisters of the abbey of Fontenay,
which was built by Saint Bernard of Clairvaux
in the twelfth century. The monks of
Fontenay ensured their self-sufficiency by
establishing a fish farm and an iron foundry
to make agricultural tools.
Within a century there were more than one
thousand Cistercian abbeys in
the Christian world.

INTRODUCTION

Inhabited since about 15,000 B.C., Burgundy is a land with a distinct identity and culture but with no easily definable borders. Today it comprises the *départements* of the Yonne, Côte d'Or, Saône-et-Loire and Nièvre, the latter being a recent addition. These *départements* are, in turn, made up of a group of diverse geographical districts or *pays*, surrounding a central mountainous and wooded area known as the Morvan.

The roots of Burgundy date back to the fifth century, when a Baltic tribe of barbarians, the Burgundii, were encouraged by the Romans to settle on the banks of the river Saône. They were dispersed in the sixth century and the Franks then took over the kingdom. In the next few centuries, through the power of the abbeys of Saint Bégnigne, Cluny and Citeaux, a vast transformation took place. Romanesque churches were built, agriculture was developed and vineyards were established. By the fifteenth century, through skilful exploitation of war, treaties, marriage and acquisition, the Duchy of Burgundy extended as far south as Provence and included most of Belgium as well as parts of the Netherlands and Switzerland. Burgundy only really became part of France in the seventeenth century. Thus, the borders of the modern *départements* bear scant resemblance to those of the Duchy.

Burgundy's long existence as a powerful centralized state is manifest in the gastronomic unity of the region, a unity maintained despite its modern division into *départements*. Traditional dishes with local variations are still made in most of Burgundy. While describing a trip through France in 1838 Stendhal noted that, 'All shades of difference are fast vanishing now in France,' and predicted that those differences would have disappeared within fifty years. Yet the particularities of each part of Burgundy are still apparent today despite the standardization that seems to be a feature of late twentieth-century life. One of the ways in which Burgundy has sought to maintain its identity has been through its cuisine.

In the distant past the mention of the word *Bourgogne* conjured up a laden table; indeed Burgundy is still best known the world over for its wines and food. A casual glance at any restaurant guide to France will show that, outside Paris, it is Burgundy which has the greatest number of fine restaurants. And yet it is surprisingly difficult to eat well and simply here except in people's homes. The tradition of the small family auberge offering uncomplicated regional dishes – the *tradition des mères* – has all but disappeared. Its decline has been brought about by rural depopulation, a shift in the routes of communication and the influence of certain economic factors: restaurants are now businesses and not supplements

Yonne

Seine

Sens

Saint-Florentin Soumaintrain
Joigny
Pontigny Tonnerre
Appoigny Auxerre Chablis Tanlay Châtillon-sur-Seine
YONNE Bailly Ancy-le-Franc
Coulanges-la-Vineuse Irancy
Toucy Noyers-sur-Serein
Fontenay Aignay-le-Duc
Saint-Sauveur-en-Puisaye Montbard Sémur-en-Auxois COTE D'OR
Serein Epoisses
Clamecy Avallon Flavigny
Vézelay Quarré-les-Tombes Ruffey
Canal du Nivernais Pierre-qui-Vire Armançon Dijon
Yonne Saulieu Canal de Bourgogne
NIEVRE Lac Pannesière Nuits-Saint-Georges Auxonne
Morvan Regional Park Arnay-le-Duc Citeaux Doubs
Château-Chinon Beaune
Nevers Meursault
Moulins-Engilbert Onlay Villapourçon Autun Santenay
Rully Pierre-de-Bresse
Saint-Léger-sous-Beuvray Le Creusot
Loire Givry Chalon-sur-Saône
Montceau-les-Mines Louhans
SAONE-ET-LOIRE Canal du Centre
Tournus
Paray-le-Monial Brancion
Charolles Cluny
Saint-Christophe-en-Brionnais La Clayette Mâcon Saône
Iguerande Chauffailles La Chapelle de Guinchay
Thoissey

WINE REGIONS

Auxerrois

Chablis

Côte de Nuits

Côte de Beaune

Côte Chalonnaise

Mâconnais

Beaujolais

- *Broken red lines indicate the departmental boundaries*
- *Broken blue lines indicate the canals*

to the family income and those that have been recently established usually offer the same newer, more sophisticated range of dishes as restaurants that have earned star rating.

Most of Burgundy is rural. There are a few cities such as Dijon and Chalon, but in between the castles, churches and abbeys are the rolling pastures of the south, green and lush even in summer; in the north, farms and plains of cereals spread as far as the eye can see.

The people of Burgundy are of mixed ancestry because this has always been a land of passage. In the past it was a halt for postal relays, and earlier this century the great restaurants made their names because they were situated on the main routes to the south of France and Italy. As soon as the *autoroute du soleil*, linking Paris with the south, was built in 1970 the region was effectively bypassed. The highway cuts the region in two and most travellers speed along it, oblivious to the more rewarding narrow roads which hug the contours of the land on either side. This has had economic consequences both for restaurateurs and wine-growers. The situation is slowly changing as a result of the judicious promotion of Burgundy's famous wines, its cultural treasures and its landscape, and the development of *fermes auberges, chambres d'hôtes* and green tourism.

In his book *The Identity of France* (1988) the French historian Fernand Braudel, writes of a journey from Beaune to Vézelay by way of Autun, passing through the Morvan, and expresses surprise at the diversity of Burgundy. In his reaction I found echoes of my own sense of surprise at its variety and at discovering the passionate pride of the people in their regional heritage. Time and time again, they stressed the notion of *terroir*, a word encompassing not just the geography but also the history and the traditions rooted in a particular territory. 'The vital thing for every community is to avoid being confused with the next tiny community, to remain other,' writes Braudel. The pride in being Burgundian is palpable, to the point where neighbouring lands which were never Burgundian, and even people who have moved to Burgundy, wish to claim its heritage. For a traveller like me, it is extraordinary to hear, even in the humblest houses of the region, tales of families with histories that go back to the fifteenth century.

In the past, commerce was facilitated by navigable rivers (the Yonne, the Seine, the Loire, the Saône and the Doubs among others) and by the construction of canals. These waterways also provided abundant freshwater fish, which were used, as they are today, in traditional fish stews cooked in wine, such as *matelote* or *pochouse* (see page 118).

A wealth of excellent produce including wines, cheese and the best meat and poultry in France (Charolais beef, Bresse chicken and pork), as well as a variety of vegetables and fruit, make up a hearty cuisine. Vegetable dishes can be innovative, but the predominant elements of Burgundian cooking tend to be meat, fish and wild mushrooms, with the addition of wine, cream, pork fat and mustard. Unusually, compared to cooking in other regions of France, spices are commonly used, especially in desserts. While some of the well-known traditional dishes are everyday fare, many have become the stuff of feasts or Sundays.

Burgundy has a long history of traditional fairs, which have become the inspiration for such new celebrations as the Foire Gastronomique de Dijon, the Charolais cattle festival in Saulieu, the snail festival at Blains Bas and the festival of the Trois Glorieuses. The latter is a celebration of wine which takes place over three days around the third weekend in

November; the climax of the Trois Glorieuses is the wine auction of the Hospices de Beaune, which takes place on a Sunday.

The product which pervades every part of Burgundy is wine. So important is it that many villages have taken on the names of the wines which they produce. Unlike the Bordelais, which comprises mainly large estates, the area under vine in Burgundy is, in general, made up of small plots. Many of these plots provide wine for personal consumption, but size is no bar to quality. This is clearly attested by vineyards such as Romanée-Conti, which produces over six thousand bottles of highly prized wine every year. The total area of vines has begun to increase but is nowhere near as extensive as it was in the last century.

Tastes in wines have changed and Burgundy now exports more white wines than red wines. Young vignerons, such as Vincent Joblot in the Côte Chalonnaise, tell me that they are only now learning how to make consistently good wine. In the past, he conjectures, good wine was achieved more by accident than by science. Henri Roch of Romanée-Conti is more inclined to give the past its due and claims that, ' ... despite our youth we are bearers of the knowledge of our forefathers.' Although output is not as abundant here as in the Bordelais, the quality is superlative. While there are essentially only three grape types – Pinot Noir for red Burgundies, Chardonnay for white wines and Gamay for Beaujolais – the complex geology and morphology of the terrain results in infinitely subtle variations of aroma and taste. In some villages everyone grows and produces wine, from the mayor to the local priest – and those who don't, wish they did.

While my original intention in writing this book was to present a straightforward chronicle of regional specialities and wines, I soon realized that I would paint a truer picture if I focused on the subject of changing trends and tastes. Many of the more traditional products of Burgundy are no longer grown, or, like asparagus in Vergigny, are produced only in tiny quantities. Others have spread to the rest of France and so have lost their regional specificity.

Nowdays most people don't have the time to cook, and the younger generation has less inclination to do so than their parents once had. On some farms it is still the grandmother who prepares the family meals, but fewer women in France are now working on the farm and this has led to a decline in rural culinary traditions. However bakeries, restaurants and delicatessens are keeping traditions alive, recreating old dishes and inventing new specialities. Changes in lifestyle are reflected in the diet. The heavy meals associated by tradition with Burgundy are now a rarity, and when they are prepared it is usually for a special occasion like a *paulée* (lunch for the farmworkers at the end of the harvest), a confirmation or a religious holiday. Many of the feast day dishes such as *boeuf bourguignon*, *coq au vin*, *jambon persillé* and *pain d'épices* have now entered the national repertoire and the phrase *'a la bourgignonne'* is used in restaurants all over the world to denote a dish cooked in a red wine sauce with a garnish of mushrooms and pearl onions.

Despite the belief of people like Dominique Rivière, director of the Eco-Musée de Bresse (charting the agricultural and gastronomic past of Bresse), that much of what is specific to Burgundy has already been lost, a positive effort is being made through public institutions such as the Conseil National des Arts Culinaires and the Morvan Regional Park to record aspects of the past before they disappear.

OPPOSITE *To my eyes, two of the most pleasing sights in any French town are the produce on display in the markets and shops, and the quaint signs which indicate the shops' wares. Many of these signs, particularly in the larger towns and cities are elaborately decorative. In Mâcon I saw a spray-painted copy of Millet's* The Gleaners *advertizing a bakery and, outside a bakery in Dijon, a small boy is depicted standing in front of a windmill with a croissant in his hand.*

But some of the most pleasing signs are those found in the smaller towns. These seem to offer a more prosaic representation of the goods on sale. The cartoon pig in Joigny and the ribboned Charolais in Paray-le-Monial (centre row) suggest uncomplicated quality.

The presentation of produce in the markets and shops almost attains the level of an art form. The way in which carrots are stacked, eggs randomly placed in a wooden box, or tomatoes made to cascade over their cartons suggests artistic sensibility and inventiveness. However it is not just the display which is so appealing; so too is the fact that one can touch and smell and make one's own choice.

From my experience of Burgundy there appeared to be fewer markets than in many other parts of France with which I am familiar, and frequently the produce on offer was not regional. But there were some markets which stood out: those of Chalon, Dijon and Mâcon. These were remarkable for the variety and quality of produce, rather than the number of stalls. Of these, Chalon was perhaps the most memorable, partly because of the pleasure of watching so many talented chefs selecting produce for their weekend menus and, afterwards, sharing a meal, and partly because the smallholders' pride in their goods was so evident.

LEFT Cherry pickers can be seen with baskets attached to their waists in order to free both hands.
RIGHT Wooden clogs on display in a sabotier's window in Saint-Père-sous-Vézelay. Once the most practical form of footwear for wet and muddy roads and fields, in recent times they have been superseded by the rubber boot. Today only a few clog-makers survive.

TOP A side door of the church of Saint Pierre in the former vigneron *quarter of Auxerre. The sixteenth-century frontispiece shows two figures with cornucopia; grapes and wheat remain two of the main products of the Auxerrois.*
ABOVE A window in Vézelay advertises the wines of the local slopes. In the reflection one can read the name of the most famous wine of northern Burgundy: Chablis.
RIGHT The moated castle of Tanlay, which was rebuilt in the sixteenth century.

L'YONNE

The approach to Burgundy from the north is gentle. Vast plains of cereals unfold before your eyes, interrupted only by the trees that gracefully line the waterways, where fishermen in emerald green boats lie in wait for pike or perch. Only when you reach the cherry orchards in the hills around Auxerre and take the small, winding road towards Chablis, see the first rows of vines, the majestic castle at Tanlay and the first hospital built at Tonnerre in the thirteenth century by Marguerite of Burgundy, to atone for the sins of her husband, do you really begin to feel that you have left the sprawling metropolis of Paris far behind.

Heading south towards Chablis from Saint-Florentin, the first abbey you encounter is one of the most spectacular: Pontigny, the largest Cistercian church in France, founded in 1114 by the followers of Saint Bernard. This religious order had one thousand five hundred abbeys by the fourteenth century and exerted a profound culinary influence on Burgundy. There is even a dish called *Saladier de Saint Bernard*, a beef daube in aspic traditionally served to grape harvesters. Despite the insistence on a simple monastic life, the bishops of Sens were said to have had special tables made to accommodate their large stomachs.

Originally the wine from Tonnerre, Chablis and the villages around Auxerre was the first to reach Paris because of the proximity of the capital. Cooking in this area is, as in the rest of Burgundy, tied to the history of the vine. Auxerre, an old gallo-Roman town on the left bank of the river Yonne, owed its prosperity to the wine trade. Saint Germain, the bishop of Auxerre in the fifth century, would offer his guests wines from his properties. Before the Revolution the wines from Auxerre were better known than any other Burgundy wine and production covered nearly two thousand hectares. Built as an amphitheatre, the medieval town centre holds many surprises, not least of which is the abbey of Saint Germain with parts dating to the eighth century. The town is also home to a fifteenth-century astronomical clock, elegant private houses of the sixteenth and seventeenth century and a breathtaking view from the Cathedral of Saint-Etienne of the varied and picturesque roofs of the city.

In the nineteenth century mildew and phylloxera devastated the vines and new railway lines were built, making the cheap wines from the Midi accessible and changing the face of agriculture. Vintners found other occupations in towns and in other types of agriculture and the ancient traditions of wine-making were gradually forgotten. All that now remains of the two thousand hectares of vines around Auxerre are three hectares of the 'Clos de la Chainette', which now belong to the psychiatric hospital of the Yonne.

In the past, throughout most of Burgundy, everything needed for the table and for animals was cultivated: wheat, oats, rapeseed, walnuts and turnips, vegetables, fruits and grapes, with the Chardonnay, the Sacy, the Melon and the Pinot Noir providing reputed wines. A pig, a cow, a few chickens and guinea fowl would provide meat, and the farmer's wife might make a little money selling eggs, milk or cheese.

While cereal cultivation is the most important economic activity in the Yonne, most farmers raise dairy cattle or pigs. There are about two hundred pig-rearing farms which yield up to fifteen per cent of the total agricultural produce of the region. Beef cattle, of which the distinctive white Charolais from the south of Burgundy is the most common, have supplanted most other races and have increased to about thirty-five thousand head.

Another change in farming has been the establishment of the large and lucrative business of farming battery-raised chickens, sold all over Europe under the name 'Duc'. Near Saint-Florentin vast white aluminium hangars signify the presence of these battery farms. Indirectly, this method of rearing chickens has had a positive effect on the production of farm-raised chickens since they are now prized as a delicacy.

Venison is provided by new deer parks, and hunting yields pheasant, partridges and quail. Blood is still used in recipes to thicken and give taste to sauces, and a traditional 'blood' pancake called *camboule* is made with deer's blood. Wild boar still roam the dense forests of the Pays d'Othe in the north-east. The eighteenth-century writer, Restif de la Bretonne, remembers eating quail and other small birds wrapped in vine leaves and cooked over hot stones. In most vine-growing areas, this remains a tradition (see recipe on page 32).

CHEESE

Among the vast plains of cereals are pasture lands dotted with small herds of Alpine Brown or Friesian cows. On good farms the cows are cosseted as much is required from them in the course of a year. Besides giving birth they must produce milk regularly and in great quantities. A single dairy cow will yield between eight and ten thousand litres of milk per year, most of which goes to cheese-making factories.

Cheese-making in the valley of the Armance was encouraged by the Cistercian monks of the abbey of Pontigny in the twelfth century. It is also mentioned in a letter of Louis XI dating back to 1479 and, though methods have changed, it continues to this day. After the Second World War there was a gradual shift from traditional to industrial methods of cheese production. This shift became so pronounced that the future of local farmhouse cheeses was put in jeopardy and associations were formed to save them. Now Soumaintrain cheese is made by several small farms, together with its fresh (not yet mature) equivalent Saint-Florentin. In the dairy of Madame Leclère, on the outskirts of Soumaintrain, I was asked to choose from trays of the round cheeses, some with pale honey-coloured ribbed rind, others darker and drier, while the newer ones were still almost rindless. Soumaintrain has a mild but pronounced flavour once it is well matured. Mixed with a little cream and spread over bread dough, it makes a delicious *tarte au Soumaintrain* (see recipe on page 31).

TOP AND ABOVE Saint Etienne cathedral dominates the river Yonne at Auxerre; Soumaintrain cheese from the valley of the river Armance.
OPPOSITE A fifteenth-century astronomical clock, built into a Roman gate in the centre of Auxerre.

SWEETS

*The huge crop of sunflowers and rapeseed
grown on the plains of the Yonne
has led to the proliferation of beekeeping.
The area was known in the last century
for the honey made by the bees
that populated the sainfoin, a crop produced
to feed horses. Attempts are now
being made to reintroduce it on a small scale.
Near the town of Joigny, north of Auxerre,
honey producer Doisnon makes pain d'épices,
and delicious meringues flavoured with
hazelnuts, almonds or coconuts
(illustrated above).
La Tentation, a local pastry shop in
Tonnerre, makes sweets known as Marguérite
de Bourgogne (illustrated below) in honour
of the founder of the town's first hospital,
which was built in the thirteenth century.*

TOP *The beautiful light-filled interior of the
basilica of Sainte Marie-Madeleine in Vézelay,
where the majestic Romanesque nave culminates
in a radiant gothic chancel.*
ABOVE *Narrow streets in Joigny descend to the river.*

DUCK SAUSAGE

Many small farms now raise ducks for foie gras and magrets *(duck breasts).*

At Le Paysan Bourguignon at Beugnon, near Saint-Florentin, Monsieur and Madame Roy, a retired truck driver and his wife, a former accountant, raise ducks. For two consecutive years they have won gold medals at the Journées Gourmandes de Saulieu, a competition for local producers (see page 40).

They make a duck sausage using only duck meat combined with walnuts or hazelnuts, and another with foie gras, which makes a lovely starter for a picnic. Their smoked and dry-cured magret *is also popular, as are duck terrines made with pistachios or cherries.*

Madame Roy suggested serving fresh foie gras with a seasonal fruit sauce, such as cherries in June or quince in the autumn.

VEGETABLES AND TRUFFLES

Vast quantities of tomatoes, cucumbers, onions and endives are produced in hothouses or vegetable gardens in the outskirts of Auxerre. Organic agriculture in Burgundy began in this district, together with the area around Beaune and its vineyards, in the 1970s. This method of farming includes the rearing of cattle and poultry, polyculture and the cultivation of market gardens and vines. It avoids the use of chemical products, uses natural compost and fertilizers and employs traditional methods of crop rotation. Burgundy is a pioneer in this field and is the only region in France to have an organic label, 'Biobourgogne', which guarantees that a product complies with specific standards approved by the Ministry of Agriculture.

South of Saint-Florentin lie the tiny villages of Vergigny and Cheu, which have not changed in size this century. In the past they specialized in the production of Argenteuil asparagus (small and white with purple tips, the spears are eaten whole) and tiny red beans, known as *coco de Cheu*, much prized because of their firm texture, taste and digestibility. The commercial production of these vegetables was aided by the building of the railway line which connected these communities with the markets of Paris. The tiny red beans of Cheu are now only cultivated on a small scale. Found on local market stalls, they are similar to the variety from Provence, and are very good in a *potée bourguignonne* or cooked in Beaujolais or a young red wine (see recipe on page 32).

Asparagus production began in 1860, and up until 1945 about fifty-five tons of asparagus were grown annually and sent to Paris by rail. Kept in damp wine cellars, the asparagus retained its taste and freshness until it was ready to be transported. The asparagus still has to be picked by hand, prized out of the earth with a long-bladed gouge rather than cut by machines. The tips and the stalk of the asparagus cut in rounds can also be served in an omelette. The flavour of the asparagus is so delicate that it should not be overpowered by a potent sauce. Since the Second World War a growth in industry has led to the gradual abandonment of many rural traditions as well as depopulation. In place of the fields of beans and asparagus one now finds plantations of young trees. These are easier to grow than asparagus and commercially more profitable.

Here, as in many parts of Burgundy, an attempt is being made by a few individuals to preserve certain traditions, resuscitate others and adapt old ways to modern methods. One such individual is Francis Marquet, a professor at the Lycée Agricole and author of an illustrated history of Saint-Florentin, who has brought new life to the community of Vergigny. He has instituted a Fête des Asperges which takes place in June and a Confrérie des Asperges de Vergigny to promote the asparagus. While these might not halt the decline in the cultivation of asparagus it is a laudable way of reminding the present generation of the agricultural past of the town.

New members of the confraternity are sworn in by the old. They wear long, mustard-yellow corduroy robes with black astrakhan-type sleeve edges, covered with purple capes. Apparently the only robes available to rent for the first ceremony of the Confrérie five years ago were of this colour and the purple capes were added to symbolize the purple tips of

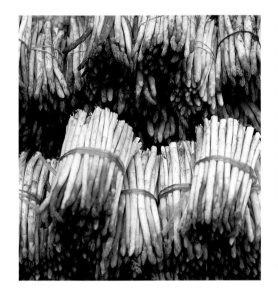

FAR LEFT, TOP Francis Marquet and two
companions in their ceremonial robes
at the ceremony of the Confrérie des
Asperges de Vergigny.
FAR LEFT, CENTRE White asparagus is a rare
delicacy which can be found in markets in June.
FAR LEFT, BOTTOM Sausages hanging up to dry
in the town of Noyers-sur-Serein.
ABOVE The red-tiled roofs of the pretty town of
Fontenailles, surrounded by wheat fields.
LEFT Cheu was once famous for growing coco
beans, displayed here on a market stall, but now
they are grown locally on a small scale.

TOP If truffles are stored with fresh eggs, they will
infuse the eggs with their unique aroma.
ABOVE The imposing church of Saint-Pierre,
dating from the twelfth century, stands
on the hill above Tonnerre.
RIGHT The church at Lucy-sur-Yonne, visible
through a frame of poplar trees.
The Canal du Nivernais was once used
to float wood downstream from the Morvan.

the asparagus. During the ceremony suggestive verses on the properties of the asparagus are sung. New members of the confraternity are bestowed with an aspargus-shaped medallion and, while eating asparagus mousse, vow to consume asparagus of Vergigny, accompanied by Chablis, every year.

There is also an annual *Fête de la Truffe* in the tiny village of Châtel Gérard in the valley of the river Serein. A range of truffles exists in Burgundy but the true Burgundy truffle (*Tuber uncinatum*) is chocolate-coloured with ivory veins. According to grower and expert Michel Jalade, this variety was the first to have graced the table of the kings of France because of the proximity of Burgundy to Paris. Although truffle production has virtually disappeared in Burgundy, truffles are still grown in the area around Tonnerre, Châtillon-sur-Seine and the Plateau de Langres. *Truffières* of oak or hazelnut trees can take up to twelve years to mature before yielding a crop. Burgundy truffles have a lighter flavour than most other varieties and must not be cooked as they lose their aroma entirely. Quite inexpensive compared to the Périgord truffle, they make a delicious and crunchy addition to a *fricassée* of wild mushrooms or to salads, pasta or marinated salmon. The president of the association of truffle growers, the restaurateur Jean-Luc Barnabet of Auxerre, offers such unusual delicacies as truffle ice-cream.

For the past twenty years Michel Jalade has been studying the mysteries of truffles in the area east of Tonnerre, near the imposing castle of Tanlay. When I met him there in June it was not the season for truffles (although the Burgundy truffle is collected earlier than the Périgord variety, if collected too early it has even less flavour than usual). However, having locked up his raucous truffle dogs, this small, wiry man was happy to show me the *truffière* in his front garden. He owns around five hundred trees for the cultivation of truffles and hunts for truffles in the Tonnerrois through four thousand hectares of forest.

Annual production is a closely guarded secret in the world of truffles and few people even admit to dealing in them. Michel Jalade's family came from Provence and used to deal in truffles, but his aged aunt never once told him how many she had found. He showed me albums of photographs charting the intricate development of truffle spores and explained that the truffle organism initially lives in symbiosis with tree roots but that later the relationship becomes a destructive one, the truffle preying upon the tree and weakening it. Truffle-growing is not easy and is not always successful.

Madame Jalade suggested a delicious salad dressing with truffles. If you soak twenty-five grams of truffles in a quarter of a litre of grapeseed oil for two days, you can then use the oil to make a dressing for a mixed salad or a salad of warm potatoes decorated with a few slices of truffle. The heady aroma and flavour of truffles is absorbed and fixed by cream, butter and milk. Keeping the truffles, together with other ingredients such as eggs, in an airtight container for twenty-four to forty-eight hours will add a delicate but distinctive truffle flavour to the dish.

The early twentieth-century novelist, Colette, who came from Saint-Sauveur-en-Puisaye, believed that one should not be parsimonious in the use of truffles: her recommendation was to cook them whole in Chablis wine with *lardons* and to serve at least one truffle per person.

GHERKINS

The fine gherkins prepared at Appoigny by the firm of Segma Liebig Maille are justly famous. About three thousand tons of them are sold per year, sixty per cent of which come from the six hundred or so local growers. Reputedly originating in India, gherkins appeared at banquets in Burgundy as early as 1583, but they made the transition from small-scale cultivation to mass market production after the ravages of phylloxera in the nineteenth century when farmers were forced to diversify their crops. The pickling varieties range from the 'extra fins' of fifteen millimetres to the 'fins' of up to nineteen millimetres. If they are over twenty-three millimetres long, they are classified as large and fetch a significantly lower price. Picked very small, they are covered with salt and, after a few hours, dried and placed in glass preserving jars. They are then covered with a litre of white wine vinegar which has been boiled with four garlic cloves, parsley, tarragon and half a dozen black peppercorns. The gherkins are ready to eat after one month and are often served with home-cured ham or pâté de campagne.

THE ORCHARDS

The outskirts of most towns of the Yonne have splendid market gardens and orchards, though I am told that it is only a few determined gardeners who continue to tend the wonderful variety of fruits and vegetables they produce: these include peas, string beans, plums, mirabelles, blackcurrants, redcurrants, strawberries, raspberries, rhubarb, apples, pears and, of course, the famous Burgundy cherries. The produce is sold by individual producers at local markets during the season or, as a charming old man told me when I met him working his plot at Coulanges-la-Vineuse, they are kept to provide the entire family with vegetables and fruits and give, as he said, 'a little pleasure'.

Market gardens also produce herbs, which are generally grown in rows bordering flowerbeds. In many markets you will find an old woman supplementing her pension by selling herbs such as sorrel, lemon balm, parsley, sage, chervil, lemon thyme, tarragon and marjoram. The herbs have obviously been picked that morning and are displayed in appealing little bunches.

A common sight in many market gardens or smallholdings are cherry trees, known as *meurisiers*, bearing sour cherries. Their fruit is the first choice of many for jam-making, for steeping in *eau de vie*, or for use in pies and *tartouillats*. The latter, a flan cooked in cabbage leaves (see recipe on page 37) is known by many different names, depending on the district – *clafoutis*, *cacous* or, in the Charolais, *tourtial*. A rustic custard dessert, it was served as a tea-time treat to children and to those bringing in the harvest. There are different methods of preparing it but experts say it is important to leave the stones in the cherries to give flavour (although not when serving to young children!). The types of cherries used also vary: some people prefer small, wild red cherries while others prefer the large black variety. The *tartouillat* is delicious made with apples, pears or redcurrants.

The slopes and limestone plateaux of the Auxerrois are good terrain for cherry trees. Cherry growing began in about the 1850s and flourished with the arrival of the railway line in the 1870s, which meant that transport to Paris was quick and easy. The trees grew to eighteen metres and had a yield of more than a ton a year. Destruction of the vines by phylloxera between 1885 and 1905 meant that farmers had to look for other means of subsistence. Just as today, the key word was diversification, and in Burgundy farmers turned to cherries which they planted like vines in parallel rows. The cherries from the region around Auxerre were well known in Paris. The Marmotte was the favourite, so-called, according to local legend, because the man who commercialized them was nicknamed Monsieur Marmotte: like a woodchuck (*Marmotte*), renowned for its sleeping habits, he always slept on the horse-drawn carriage which took him to his orchards.

The cultivation of the Marmotte cherry at the turn of the century was a great success; its large, shiny fruit is sweet and heart-shaped, with a line running through the middle. Today cherry production is in decline. This is partly due to the increase in acreage devoted to vines, which provide a greater financial return, but also due to the expense of harvesting cherries and their lack of durability. They must be picked ripe by hand so as not to bruise them, and must be brought to the consumer within, at most, a day of picking.

TOP Flowers sold in local markets are often grown as colourful borders to vegetable gardens. ABOVE A market garden by the river Serein. OPPOSITE TOP Varieties of cider apple grown by Philippe Charlois in his Pays d'Othe orchard. OPPOSITE BELOW Orchards near Coulanges-la-Vineuse.

RATAFIA

The view from the orchards of the plateau of the
Pays d'Othe, overlooking the plain of
Saint-Florentin, is spectacular.
With one hundred and fifty different apple
varieties, this area was once a greater producer
of cider than Normandy.
Philippe and Florence Charlois, a young couple
who have taken over Philippe's father's
farm near Champion, have bought and revived
old orchards nearby and are producing
cider using an ancient pressoir.
They also make apple marc in the antique
family still, and ratafia.
An old Burgundian speciality, ratafia is a
traditional country aperitif made by
the maceration of fruits in alcohol.
Usually made with cherries, raspberries or
blackcurrants, it is similar to the crème de cassis
now made commercially.
It can be a mixture of grape juice and
marc or, as in the Pays d'Othe, apple juice, cider
and apple marc. Ratafia has between sixteen
and eighteen degrees of alcoholic volume.

In the hills around Coulanges-la-Vineuse Jean-Yves Lemoule and his Tahitian wife pick cherries in the cool of the early morning in order to have them ready for the local markets and supermarkets. They employ about thirty seasonal pickers, many of whom have been with the Lemoule family since Jean-Yves took over his parents' farm ten years ago. Wearing baskets tied to their waists, the pickers carefully select the ripe fruit. Those who pick fruit which is either too ripe or not sufficiently mature are scolded by the ever-vigilant Lemoules. This is a more difficult operation than it might at first appear, for it is important not to break branches or to dislodge any of the immature fruit. Varieties grown here include Marmotte, Noire Brûlat, Hedelfingen, Starking and Van for eating and Early for jams. The season lasts for only a few weeks. The Lemoule farm comprises fifteen hectares of cherry orchards, eight hectares of vines and fifty hectares of wheat, rapeseed and peas for animal feed.

Around the commune of Escolives-Saint-Camille, the site of some extraordinary Roman finds, local cherry producers have established a small market. Escolives holds a cherry festival around the last weekend in June, where a prize is awarded to the best producer. The Lemoules have received two trophies but no longer have the time to compete. The merits of different types of cherry are hotly discussed, and everyone has his or her favourite variety.

There are about forty varieties of cherries which are subjected to various tests at the national research laboratory at Bordeaux. Once they have been tested for taste, durability, consumer reaction, resistance to weather and disease, and ease of picking, the most suitable are retained. According to Daniel Moiron, researcher at the Lycée Agricole of Champ-sur-Yonne, the least hardy but perhaps most delicious varieties may be abandoned forever.

THE VINEYARDS

Established in 1935, L'Institut National des Appellations d'Origine (INAO) is the body which controls the quality of wine and food in France by issuing a guarantee of origin, an *appellation d'origine contrôlée* (AOC). Each product is regulated by a separate law which states that its place of origin must be identified and that methods of production must be consistent with certain established local criteria. For wine this means that the grape variety, the proportion of the grape used if the wine is blended, the location and yield of the vineyard, the alcoholic strength of the wine and the methods of cultivation and vinification must all conform to specific standards in order to merit the AOC label.

Rules change according to the state of current techniques and yields may be modified each year upon special request by the vignerons, who apply to the INAO. The list of wines and foods awarded an AOC grows each year.

All wines are divided into four basic groups: *vin de table, vin de pays, vin de qualité supérieure* and AOC. AOCs in Burgundy are in turn divided into *grand crus* (which comprise only one per cent of total production), *appellations communales premiers crus* or *villages premiers crus* (together making up eleven per cent of production), *appellations communales* (twenty-three per cent) and *appellations régionales* (sixty-five per cent). If a classified wine falls below the standards required of its grade, it is demoted to a lesser *appellation* until it once again achieves its previous quality.

OPPOSITE LEFT, RIGHT AND ABOVE Picking and sorting cherries grown in the orchards of the Lemoules outside Coulanges-la-Vineuse.
This pretty village, which owes its name to the extensive vineyards around it, still has a magnificent eighteenth-century pressoir.
Legend has it that, during a fire in the seventeenth century, wine was used to quell the flames as it was a great deal more abundant than water.
ABOVE Vineyards on the slopes outside Irancy. Vines have been grown on these slopes since Roman times and the principal vine type, César or Romain, reflects this heritage. A difficult grape from which to make consistently good wines, it is slowly being replaced by the Pinot Noir, the classic red Burgundy grape. In 1977 Irancy was given the right to label its wines 'Bourgogne Irancy'.

TOP The twelfth-century church of the abbey of Pontigny, built by Cistercian monks who owned and tended the Chablis vineyards by the river Serein.

ABOVE AND TOP RIGHT Chablis wines now cover over three thousand hectares in the valley of the river Serein. A dry white wine made from the Chardonnay grape variety, Chablis is light with a delicate perfume and a clear, golden green colour.

RIGHT The last lock of the Canal du Nivernais shortly before it joins the river Yonne near Auxerre.

There is an obsession with wines in Burgundy. Initially bemused and quite unsure of what all the fuss was about, I soon became fascinated; a visit to a wine-maker is truly one of the great experiences of Burgundy and of France. Entering a wine-maker's dim and fragrant cellar, one has a sense of penetrating a mysterious inner sanctum and of discovering one man's personal philosophy. There is no doubt that wine-making is an intense passion and nowhere is this passion more apparent than in Burgundy.

The characteristic feature of wine-growing in Burgundy is that properties are small. Most wine-makers believe it is essential to work in the vineyards and cellars themselves. Once the property becomes too big, it requires an administrator to run it.

Before the phylloxera epidemic of the mid-nineteenth century the northern *pays* had the largest quantity of vines in all of Burgundy (over forty thousand hectares) and more than thirty varieties of grape. This was not just because the local climate and the terrain were particularly suited to the vine, but, because of northern Burgundy's proximity to thirsty Paris. The barrels of wine were transported by barge, sharing passage with wood from the Morvan and limestone for the construction of buildings in the capital. Wine was also sent on to England, Belgium and Holland.

As far back as the twelfth century the Abbey of Pontigny was making wines in Chablis and some *clos* (walled vineyards) date back to the seventh century. References to these are found in the archives of abbeys to which the king had donated lands for the cultivation of vines.

The majority of wines from northern Burgundy now come from the *appellation* of Chablis. There are four categories: the *grand crus* cover about one hundred hectares, the *premiers crus* seven hundred hectares, Chablis itself two thousand three hundred hectares and the Petit Chablis three hundred and sixty hectares. The area under vines has expanded dramatically in the past few years (less than thirty years ago the Chablis wine-growing area covered only sixty hectares). This expansion has taken place partly because the profits on vines are greater than on food crops and partly because the area delimited as Chablis has been enlarged.

Chablis is now a household name and one of the most famous wines in the world. The best Chablis, the *grand crus,* have not changed since the creation of the *appellation d'origine contrôlée* in 1938. The Chablis grape type is the Chardonnay, and the best soil for its cultivation is believed to be Kimmeridgian limestone, on which the town of Chablis is built. Expanding the acreage of the *appellation* has meant that the villages using the name Chablis are ever more distant from Chablis itself and that the soil type is no longer confined to Kimmeridgian. Problems such as frost mean that production can fluctuate greatly, but the demand is constant and this is reflected in its high price.

With properties small and production uneven in the cold weather of northern Burgundy, it is an onerous task for producers to make, bottle and distribute their wine. In many areas growers have pooled their resources and formed cooperatives. Cave 'la Chablisienne', located in Chablis and started in 1923, does not own a winepress: it receives the pressed grapes from its members, then makes and markets the wine. A variety of consistently good wines are produced of which Vieilles Vignes 1991 is excellent, as are the Chablis of 1989 and 1993.

CREMANT DE BAILLY

An unusual kind of wine-tasting experience can be enjoyed at the village of Bailly on the banks of the river Yonne, close to the wine-producing hills south of Auxerre. Limestone was quarried here in the twelfth century and the quarries which were closed in 1914 and used initially for growing mushrooms were converted into wine cellars in 1972. Coming in from the heat of the summer sun, the coolness of the cellars is quite welcoming and the line-up of over four million Crémant bottles stocked in large vaults is an impressive sight. A huge bar offers tastings to visitors. As for other sparkling Burgundys, Crémant de Bailly is produced by the méthode champenoise, *from a variety of grapes of which Pinot Noir and Chardonnay must form the base. The fermented juice is bottled and the addition of sugar produces a second fermentation. The bottles are aged for several years and turned at intervals before they are frozen in order to extract the sediment. Sparkling white or rosé Burgundy achieved* appellation *status in 1975.*

L'ESPERANCE

89450 SAINT-PERE-SOUS-VEZELAY, TEL 86 33 20 45

At Saint-Père-sous-Vézelay stands l'Espérance, a delightful hotel and restaurant run by Marc Meneau, one of the great chefs of France. Born near Saint-Père, he has remained true to his Burgundy roots, allowing the seasons to dictate his menus and transforming regional dishes to suit more sophisticated palates. Marc Meneau's cooking could be described as baroque: it is rich, ornate and inventive. He points out that a cook, like a painter, must constantly reinvent dishes. Monsieur Meneau explains that he likes to drink a great wine either on its own or to accompany a simple dish, and to drink a simple wine with an exceptional dish in order not to overwhelm the palate. As he points out, a meal cannot have two winners.

CREME DE NOIX

Walnut Cream Soup

A delicious and easy starter for a cold autumn day, especially when fresh walnuts are in season in October. (Illustrated above)

SERVES 4-6
200g/7oz fresh walnut halves, blanched
100ml/3½ fl oz chicken stock
500ml/16fl oz single cream
salt and freshly ground black pepper
100ml/3 ½ fl oz whipping cream
55g/2oz chopped fresh walnuts

Mix the walnuts and the stock in a medium saucepan, then simmer to reduce the stock by two-thirds. Stir in the single cream and bring to the boil, then simmer until the soup has thickened slightly. Season to taste with salt and freshly ground black pepper.

In the meantime, beat the whipping cream until soft peaks form.

To serve, pour the soup into soup plates, cover with 1 tablespoon of whipped cream and sprinkle with chopped walnuts.

ANGUILLES AU LAURIER

Eel Marinated in Bay Leaves
(Illustrated right)

SERVES 4
1.5kg/3 ½ lb eel, cut into 4cm/1 ½ in slices

FOR THE MARINADE
1 garlic head, separated into cloves
500ml/16fl oz olive oil
4 bay leaves

FOR THE SAUCE
1 garlic head, separated into cloves
400ml/14fl oz roast beef juices or beef stock
100ml/3 ½ fl oz olive oil
juice of 1 lemon
1tbsp butter, diced
salt and freshly ground black pepper

Prepare the marinade a day in advance. Blanch the garlic cloves in boiling water. Add the cloves to the olive oil together with the bay leaves and let the mixture cool. Put the eel in a large bowl and cover with the marinade. Leave to marinate overnight in the refrigerator.

Preheat the oven to 110°C/230°F/gas mark ¼.

To make the sauce, slice the garlic cloves thinly. Blanch them in boiling water for 1 minute. Whisk the roast beef juices with the oil and lemon juice in a saucepan and season. Add the garlic and cook gently to heat through.

Take the eel out of the marinade and put in an oven-proof dish. Discard the marinade, reserving the bay leaves for garnish. Cover the eel with the sauce and bake for 15 minutes until tender. Pour off the sauce into a saucepan and cover the eel with foil. Whisk the butter into the sauce and season.

Pour the sauce over the eel and garnish with the bay leaves.

GOUGERES

Choux Pastries with Cheese

These pastries originate in Tonnerre but a Flemish version with cheese sprinkled on top and a pastry by the name of goyère is mentioned in thirteenth-century French texts. Gougères are usually served with Chablis as a snack. You will find them all over Burgundy in bakeries and charcuteries, but they are very easy to make at home. You can substitute dried goats' cheese for the Gruyère. (Illustrated left)

MAKES 24 PASTRIES
125g/4 ½ oz butter, diced
½ tsp salt
pinch of cayenne pepper
pinch of grated nutmeg
115g/4oz plain flour, sifted
4 eggs
**115g/4oz Gruyère or Comté cheese,
finely diced**

Preheat the oven to 200°C/400°F/gas mark 6.

Mix 250ml/8fl oz of water, the butter, salt, cayenne and nutmeg in a saucepan and bring to the boil. Remove the pan from the heat and add the flour all at once, beating vigorously until the mixture leaves the sides of the pan.

Leave the mixture to cool slightly, then whisk in the eggs, one at a time, whisking after each addition until the mixture is thick and glossy. Beat in the diced cheese and mix well.

Drop the mixture, one tablespoon at a time, on to a well-greased baking sheet.

Bake for 15 minutes, then lower the oven temperature to 180°C/350°F/gas mark 4 and bake for a further 15 minutes or until golden. The *gougères* should be crisp on the outside and soft and moist on the inside. Leave to cool on a wire rack.

SALADE VIGNERONNE

Dandelion Leaves with Bacon and Red Wine Vinegar Dressing

The best wild dandelions are reputed to be found growing next to molehills. For a salad such as this one, it is best to choose the small tender inner dandelion leaves. In the Beaujolais region, a variation of this salad is made with the addition of chopped hard-boiled eggs and tomatoes.

SERVES 4
140g/5oz smoked back bacon, with the rind removed
115g/4oz young dandelion leaves or salade frisée
115g/4oz lamb's lettuce
115g/4oz cooked beetroot, diced
1tbsp walnut oil
2tbsp red wine vinegar
2tsp fresh chives, finely chopped
salt and freshly ground black pepper

Put the bacon in a small saucepan, cover with water and bring slowly to the boil. Drain and cut into thin strips.

Rinse the dandelion leaves and the lamb's lettuce in several changes of cold water, then dry them well in paper towels. Place them in a large salad bowl and sprinkle the beetroot over the top.

Sauté the bacon in the walnut oil in a small frying pan for 2-3 minutes. Put the bacon strips in the salad bowl and scrape the juices from the frying pan over the salad.

Return the frying pan to the heat and pour in the vinegar. When the vinegar comes to the boil, pour it over the salad. Mix well and season to taste. Sprinkle the chives over the salad and serve immediately.

TARTE AU SOUMAINTRAIN

Soumaintrain Cheese Tart

In the village of Soumaintrain the production of the local cheese, with its golden yellow rind, had ceased until the Chamber of Agriculture stepped in with funds. The cheese is now made in several farmhouses. If you cannot find Soumaintrain, substitute Chaumes, a similar cheese from the Dordogne with a washed rind.

SERVES 4-6
1½ tsp dried yeast
2½ tbsp vegetable oil
1tsp salt
350g/12oz plain flour

FOR THE FILLING
6tbsp single cream
250g/8 ½ oz Soumaintrain cheese, thinly sliced, with the rind
salt and freshly ground black pepper

To make the pastry, dissolve the yeast in 200ml/7fl oz of tepid water in a large bowl. Then add 1 ½ tablespoons of the oil, the salt and the flour and mix to form a soft but not sticky dough. Add more flour if necessary.

Turn out the dough on to a lightly floured surface and knead for 10 minutes until very smooth and elastic. Put the dough back in the bowl, cover, and leave in a warm place to rise for about 1 hour, until it has doubled in bulk.

Preheat the oven to 250°F/475°C/gas mark 9. Grease two 28 x 22.5cm/11 x 9in baking trays.

Divide the dough in half and roll each half out on a lightly floured surface until it is very thin. Transfer the dough sheets to the baking trays and trim to fit. Spread the cream over the sheets, leaving a 1cm/ ½ in border uncovered.

Dot with the cheese and season.

Bake for 20 minutes, checking several times. Cover with foil if the cheese is browning too quickly. Slice and serve hot as a luncheon dish with a salad or as an aperitif.

GRATIN DE POMMES DE TERRE AUX TRUFFES

Potato Gratin with Truffles

Potato gratins such as this one are served all over Burgundy.

SERVES 4
30g/1oz truffles, fresh or bottled (optional)
150ml/5fl oz cream
2kg/4 ½ lb baking potatoes, peeled and thinly sliced
125g/4 ½ oz Gruyère cheese, grated
600ml/21fl oz milk
175g/6½ oz butter, diced
salt and freshly ground black pepper

Preheat the oven to 180°C/350°F/gas mark 4 and lightly grease a 25.5cm/10in oven-proof serving dish.

Using the slicing part of a grater, shave half of the truffles into very thin slices. Set aside. Dice the remaining truffles. If you have used bottled truffles, mix 2 teaspoons of truffle juice with the cream in a small mixing bowl.

Layer half of the potatoes in the dish. Pour over the milk and sprinkle with the diced truffles and half of the cheese. Layer the remaining potatoes and finish with the rest of the cheese and diced butter. Season the cream with salt and pepper and pour over the top.

Bake for 1 ½ hours, covering the dish with foil for the first 30 minutes. Serve with the truffles shavings sprinkled over the top.

CAILLES ROTIES DANS DES FEUILLES DE VIGNES AVEC DES RAISINS

Quails Roasted in Vine Leaves with Red and White Grapes

This dish can be made with a variety of different birds, such as partridges, pheasants, guinea fowl and chicken. It is always a success at dinner parties.

SERVES 4
8 oven-ready quails
8 large fresh vine leaves, rinsed; or vine leaves preserved in brine, soaked overnight and rinsed
8 slices of barding fat
55g/2oz butter
200ml/7fl oz dry white Burgundy wine
1tbsp marc or brandy
85g/3oz shallots, finely chopped
400g/14oz mixed red and white grapes, peeled and seeded
salt and freshly ground black pepper

Truss the quails and wrap each one in a vine leaf, then cover with a slice of barding fat.

Melt the butter in a large frying pan and sauté the birds for 3 minutes on each side. Lower the heat, cover and cook for 8 minutes. Remove the birds, cover and set aside.

Pour the wine and marc into the frying pan, add the shallots and simmer for 5 minutes. Add the grapes, cover and simmer for 2 minutes, then transfer the grapes to a bowl and cover to keep warm. Return the quails to the frying pan and simmer for 1 minute on each side.

Serve 2 quails per person covered with the sauce and surrounded by the grapes.

COCO DE CHEU A LA VIGNERONNE

Coco Beans Cooked in Red Wine

As wine is readily available and relatively inexpensive in Burgundy it is common to cook with young wine or leftovers. The local coco beans are known for their delicate taste, but use kidney or pinto beans as a substitute. (Illustrated above)

SERVES 4
450g/1lb dried *coco* beans
1 large onion
2 cloves
250g/8½oz belly of pork or back bacon
400ml/14fl oz full-bodied red wine
1 bouquet garni
2 garlic cloves
salt and freshly ground black pepper
2tbsp finely chopped fresh parsley

Rinse the beans, place in a large pan, cover with water and leave to soak overnight. Drain, then return them to the rinsed pan, add water to cover and boil hard for 10 minutes. Drain again and return to the rinsed pan. Add the onion studded with the cloves, the bacon, half the wine, 400ml/14fl oz of water, the bouquet garni and the garlic cloves.

Cover and simmer gently for about 2 hours or until the beans are tender. Add the remaining wine after 1½ hours and add a little more water if necessary. The mixture should not be completely dry at the end of the cooking time.

Before serving, use a knife and fork to cut the bacon into small pieces, add salt and pepper and decorate with the parsley.

MAGRETS DE CANARD AUX BAIES DE CASSIS ET AUX POIRES

Duck Breasts with Blackcurrants and Pears

The abundance of blackcurrants in Burgundy leads to a variety of delicious sweet and savoury dishes cooked with this fruit. If the duck breasts are fairly large you will only need one half per person. Serve with wild rice or red Camargue rice. (Illustrated right)

SERVES 4
4 whole duck breasts
4 Comice pears, peeled, cored and cut into quarters
200ml/7fl oz red wine, such as Beaujolais
1 clove
½ cinnamon stick
1 ½ tbsp honey
250g/8 ½ oz blackcurrants
4tbsp crème de cassis

Sauté the duck breasts in batches, skin side down first, for 8 minutes on each side in a dry frying pan. You can cook for less time for pink breasts, or more for well done, according to taste. Remove from the pan, cover and set aside. Discard most of the fat from the pan.

Put the wine, spices and honey in a pan. Add the pears and poach for 5-10 minutes until tender but still holding their shape.

Add the wine to the frying pan and simmer for 5 minutes stirring occasionally.

Stir in the pears, the blackcurrants and the crème de cassis, then return the breasts to the pan and simmer for a further 5 minutes.

Remove the breasts, slice thinly and arrange on plates. Garnish with the pears and sauce.

L'OIE DU CHAMPION

Goose Stuffed with Apples

This recipe comes from Philippe and Florence Charlois, apple growers in the Pays d'Othe, and uses apples and cider from this region. The ideal accompaniments are apple jelly, chestnut purée (see page 117) and roast potatoes.

SERVES 6-8

4.5kg/10lb young goose with giblets
2 onions, finely chopped
2 bacon rinds
3 leeks, chopped
3 carrots, chopped
750ml/27fl oz cider
1 bouquet garni
1 celery stalk, chopped
1 egg yolk

FOR THE STUFFING

2 onions, finely chopped
1tbsp goose fat or vegetable oil
4 small apples, peeled, cored and diced
1tsp ground cinnamon or allspice
3tbsp apple marc or calvados
1 goose liver, taken from giblets, finely chopped
250g/8½oz bacon, rinded and very finely chopped
250g/8½oz pork fillet, minced or very finely chopped
1 slice day-old bread
2 eggs, beaten
1tsp oil for frying
salt and freshly ground black pepper

To prepare the stuffing, fry the onions in the goose fat or vegetable oil until they are translucent, then stir in the apples and fry for a further 2 minutes. Sprinkle the cinnamon and 2 tablespoons of the apple marc over the apples and onions. Remove from the heat and leave to cool.

Preheat the oven to 230°C/450°F/gas mark 8.

Combine the goose liver with the chopped bacon and pork fillet. Soak the bread in the remaining marc, pour over the eggs and then process in a food processor. Mix in the chopped meat, onions and apples. In a small frying pan, fry a tablespoon of the mixture in the oil and taste to check the seasoning. Add salt and freshly ground black pepper, and more cinnamon and upto 1 tablespoon of marc to the raw stuffing according to taste.

Rub the goose breast with salt and prick all over to let the fat run free while it is roasting. Stuff the goose and stand it on a rack in a large roasting tin to let the fat drain off.

Roast the goose for about 45 minutes or until it is browned. Spoon off and reserve as much fat as you can while it is roasting.

Towards the end of the roasting time, melt one tablespoon of the reserved goose fat in a sauté pan over a medium heat and sauté the onions, the giblets, bacon rinds, leeks and carrots until the onions are transluscent. Add the cider. Bring to the boil, then cover and simmer the sauce for 15 minutes.

Remove from the oven and pour the sauce around the goose in the tin. Add the bouquet garni and the celery, cover with foil and return to the oven for 1-1½ hours more, spooning off fat as necessary.

The goose is cooked when the juices run clear when the thickest part of a thigh is pierced with a knife. Drain the cooking juices from the tin and return the goose to the turned-off oven to keep warm. Skim off the fat from the juices. Bring to the simmer and whisk in the egg yolk to thicken the sauce. Taste and adjust the seasoning if necessary. Serve the goose on a bed of vegetables.

FAISAN AU CIDRE ET AUX FRUITS D'AUTOMNE

Pheasant Cooked with Cider and Autumn Fruits

(Illustrated opposite)

SERVES 4

1.35kg/3lb pheasant, plucked and drawn
4 bacon rashers
55g/2oz butter
85g/3oz shelled walnut halves
250ml/8fl oz dry cider
2tbsp marc
115g/4oz crème fraîche
55g/2oz sultanas
2 quinces or eating apples, peeled, cored and cut into quarters
salt and freshly ground black pepper

Season the bird inside and out, then truss it and cover the breasts with the bacon rashers.

Melt the butter in a large, deep frying pan or flame-proof casserole, add the bird, walnuts, cider, marc and crème fraîche. Cover and simmer for 45 minutes, turning the bird over once, half-way through the cooking time.

Meanwhile, soak the sultanas in hot water and leave to soak for 30 minutes.

Preheat the oven to 200°C/400°F/gas mark 6.

Add the drained sultanas and quince to the frying pan and continue simmering, uncovered, for a further 15 minutes. Using a slotted spoon, transfer the pheasant to an oven-proof dish and brown in the preheated oven for 10 minutes. Meanwhile, bring the sauce to the boil over a high heat for about 2-3 minutes until reduced and thickened. Season to taste. Serve surrounded by the walnuts, sultanas and quince or apple quarters with the sauce spooned over the top.

TOURTE BOURGUIGNONNE

Pork and Veal Pie

This pie is served all over northern Burgundy on feast days, and is delicious for a picnic. Serve with a watercress salad and gherkins.

SERVES 4

250g/8½oz pork, cut into 5cm/2in pieces
250g/8½oz veal, cut into 5cm/2in pieces
2 whole onions
1 garlic clove, crushed
4 sprigs of fresh thyme
1tbsp marc
300ml/10fl oz white wine
400g/14oz puff pastry, thawed if frozen
small bunch of fresh parsley
1 egg yolk, lightly beaten
½ packet good-quality aspic (optional)
salt and freshly ground black pepper

The day before, place the pork, veal, whole onions, garlic, thyme, marc and seasoning in a large non-metallic bowl. Add the wine, cover and chill overnight, stirring occasionally.

Preheat the oven to 180°C/350°F/gas mark 4.

Roll out the puff pastry on a lightly-floured surface until it is 0.5cm/¼in thick. Cut out a round or oval large enough to line the bottom and sides of a deep 20cm/8in pie dish. Roll out the remaining pastry to make a round or oval big enough to cover the pie dish and set aside.

Drain the meat from the marinade and reserve one onion. Discard the remaining onion and the thyme (keep the liquid if you intend to serve the pie cold). Pat the meat dry.

Finely chop half the meat with the onion and the parsley then alternate layers of meat with minced meat in the pie dish, starting with the minced meat.

Brush the edges of the pastry with beaten egg yolk, then add the pastry lid and press together to seal. Make a hole in the centre of the pie and insert a pie funnel made of baking paper or kitchen foil. Glaze the surface of the pie with the remaining beaten egg yolk. Bake for 45 minutes until golden brown.

You can either serve the pie hot or leave it to cool. To eat it cold, boil the reserved marinade until reduced by half. While the liquid is still hot stir in the aspic, mixing well. Strain this mixture through a fine sieve, then pour the liquid through the pie funnel, while the pie is still hot. Leave the pie to cool on a wire rack. When cool, refrigerate overnight or for at least 12 hours. The aspic will bind the meat together.

GATEAU DE MERINGUE AUX NOISETTES ET AU CHOCOLAT

Hazelnut Meringue Cake with Chocolate

Inspired by delicious honey meringues eaten in Joigny, this recipe is a delight for children. You can either cover the meringue with chocolate sauce or make a topping with crème fraîche and red fruits.

SERVES 4-6

200g/7oz walnuts halves or hazelnuts with the skins removed, coarsely chopped
6 egg whites
pinch of salt
170g/6oz sugar
1tsp honey
½tsp vanilla essence
1tsp white wine vinegar

1½tbsp plain flour
2tsp butter, for greasing

FOR THE CHOCOLATE SAUCE
115g/4oz chocolate
55g/2oz butter, softened
2 egg yolks

FOR THE RED FRUIT FINISH
200ml/7fl oz crème fraîche or whipping cream
225g/8oz red fruits, such as raspberries, strawberries and redcurrants
1tbsp sugar

Preheat the oven to 180°C/350°F/gas mark 4. Prepare a *moule à manqué* tin by buttering it and lining the bottom and sides with rice paper or baking parchment.

Toast the nuts in the oven for 10 minutes, turning over frequently. Allow to cool.

Beat the eggs with an electric mixer until they form soft peaks, then beat in the salt and sugar until the mixture is stiff. Beat in the vanilla and vinegar. Mix the nuts and flour together, then fold them into the meringue together with the honey. Spoon the meringue into the prepared tin

Bake for 1½hours until crisp and firm. Remove from the oven and leave to cool. While the meringue cools it will sink in the middle and it becomes very chewy.

To make the chocolate sauce, melt the chocolate with the butter in a heat-proof bowl placed over a saucepan of simmering water. When the chocolate has melted, take off the heat and whisk in the egg yolks, beating until smooth. Pour over the meringue to cover.

If you want to finish the meringue with red fruit instead, beat the crème fraîche or whipping cream until thick and pour over the meringue. Scatter the fruits over the top.

TARTOUILLAT

Cherry Cake

Tartouillat, clafoutis *or* flamusse *are all names
for types of tarts or flans served in Burgundy
and throughout most of France. One version of*
tartouillat *calls for them to be baked in cabbage
leaves – a practical way of making an
individual portion to eat in the vineyards. This
is more like a cake than the rustic version
which resembles a thick custard. It can be
made with cherries, apples or pears.
(Illustrated right)*

SERVES 4-6
225g/8oz plain flour
85g/3oz sugar
1 sachet (7.5g/1 ⅔ tsp) vanilla sugar
1tsp baking powder
3 eggs
3tbsp milk
75g/2 ½ oz unsalted butter, melted
900g/2lb black cherries, apples or pears

Sift the flour with the sugar into a bowl, then
stir in the vanilla sugar and baking powder
and make a well in the centre. Whisk in the
eggs and the milk to form a smooth batter.
Add 4 tablespoons of the butter. Let the batter
stand for 30 minutes while preparing the fruit.

Pit the black cherries or peel, core and
thinly slice the apples or pears.

Meanwhile, preheat the oven to
230°C/450°F/gas mark 8. Butter a 20cm/8in
round cake tin.

Stir the fruit into the batter and pour into the
buttered tin. Bake for 30 minutes or until a
skewer inserted in the centre comes out clean.
Allow to cool in the tin for about 5 minutes,
then turn out on to a wire rack and serve
warm or cold.

FAR LEFT *Logging was a traditional occupation of the Morvandiaux. The logs were transported along the rivers Yonne and Cure to Paris.*
LEFT *Fairs and feast days, dancing and colourful costumes have been part of life in the Morvan for centuries. The traditions they mark are being maintained by local groups who are keen to ensure their survival.*
RIGHT *Highly-prized ceps gathered from the forests of the Morvan.*

ABOVE *The spectacular cathedral of Saint Lazare in Autun is famed for its Romanesque sculptures, signed by the artist Gislebertus who lived and worked in the city during the early part of the twelfth century. The tympanum above the west door depicts a vivid scene from the Last Judgement: in the centre is the mandorla of Christ, to the left are the damned and to the right are the saints and the saved.*
RIGHT *Cows graze peacefully in the gently rolling meadows of the Morvan hills.*

LE MORVAN

An anomaly in the middle of fertile Burgundy, the small area known as the Morvan (Celtic for the Black Mountain) is poor, wild and sparsely populated. Inhospitable mountains and forests of beech, oak and pine isolate the tiny towns. White Charolais cattle have replaced the red Morvandelle breed, while goats and sheep graze among wild pear and apple trees.

Nowhere in Burgundy is rural depopulation as apparent as in the Morvan. 'It has lost over fifty per cent of its population and today only the wildlife seems really at home there,' wrote Fernand Braudel in *The Identity of France*. But for those accustomed to the stress of urban life the rugged and empty landscape of the Morvan has considerable appeal. This has been recognized and promoted by the Morvan Regional Park, which has encouraged the development of green tourism by providing cycle tracks, hiking and pony trekking routes. The Park authority is the primary institution responsible not only for conservation of flora and fauna but also for the promotion and study of cultural and culinary traditions. As in the rest of Burgundy, farms and crafts centres in the Morvan are opening their doors to tourists. Several *fermes auberges* now exist here, and local fare can be sampled in *chambres d'hôtes*.

The Morvan has always offered its inhabitants a scant living. Large numbers of Morvandiaux have had to leave in order to find work in nearby areas or further afield. Some, known as *galvachers* (a corruption of the word '*voyages*', meaning 'journeys') used their oxen and carts to transport wine and logs to distant towns in the spring and then sold their oxen on the way home in the autumn. When leaving Anost on May 1st, townspeople would gather in the last inn before the Morvan forest to wish the travellers a safe journey. There is now a festival and a museum of *galvachers* in Anost. The women of the region went to Paris as wet nurses or, conversely, children from Paris were sent to be raised by families in the Morvan. There is still very little industry and small farms employ twenty-six per cent of the local population compared to seven and a half per cent in the rest of Burgundy.

When the forests of Normandy were depleted by Paris, the capital turned to the Morvan and when the sale of wood became the most important source of income in the area all clearing of land stopped. Agriculture has never been easy in this highland granite region; there are no grapes and the land is not suitable for cereals. The Morvan is, however, famous for the rearing of Charolais cattle, which are sold young in markets such as the one at Moulins Engilbert, to be fattened in richer pastures in other regions of France.

The fierce attachment of the people of the Morvan to local traditions is apparent in their

ABOVE The great cathedral of Saint Lazare rising above the houses of Autun. A walled roman town, Autun once had an important Graeco-Roman academy and the largest amphitheatre in Gaul.
TOP Local bakeries and pastry shops offer a delectable assortment of breads, brioches and pastries as well as sweets, chocolates and ice-creams.

songs, dances and cooking. One traditional song refers to the eggs that are broken to prepare the famous Morvandelle omelette (made with dry-cured ham and mushrooms). Many Burgundian recipes have a Morvandelle element, though traditional dishes such as *crapiaux* (see recipe on page 54) are eaten less and less.

A traditional mainstay of the Morvan diet was bread, which was regarded with some reverence; the lending of a 'sourdough starter' (used in place of yeast) to a neighbour symbolized good relations between lender and recipient. Local 'sourdough' bread was made from any available grain, and many bakeries and most restaurants now offer a version of this bread. It is delicious with smoked fish or cheeses (see recipe on page 61).

Although there are few cities in the Morvan, there are many small and interesting towns on the outskirts of the regional park. Autun, in the south-east, was a cultural capital during the Roman empire. A theatre, a temple and Roman gates are a few of the many monuments which can be visited. At the top of a hill in the old town, the spectacular cathedral of Saint Lazare contains some of the most enchanting Romanesque sculptures in Burgundy.

To the north, commanding an imposing site above the tumultuous Cousin river, is the graceful walled town of Avallon. This town plays an important part in the commercial activities of the northern Morvan and the Yonne. Further south lies the austere town of Saulieu, built around the basilica of Saint Andoch, whose sculpted pillars are among the most beautiful in all Burgundy. Once a prosperous town, it suffered in the nineteenth century as a result of the rural exodus. Today, Saulieu is once again a gastronomic capital and the site of large country and gastronomic fairs such as the Journées Gourmandes and the Fête du Charolais.

The beauty of the Morvan is such that many people are fighting to keep the region alive. A number of the its most ardent supporters have created an organization called Artisans Producteurs et Artistes du Morvan, promoting local products and culture and offering gourmet tours and visits to museums, churches and lakes of the area.

THE STREAMS AND LAKES

The Morvan abounds in streams teeming with trout, but the rarest and most sought-after inhabitant of these waters is the wild crayfish. Once the Morvan was famous for them but now they have practically disappeared, killed off by overfishing and a virus carried by a new breed of crayfish introduced from America. Many Morvandiaux have told me that they remember when wild crayfish were so abundant that they could almost be scooped up by hand from the streams. Though the crayfish have been encouraged to breed, they have not fared well in trials. The fishing season for crayfish is now confined to one week during the month of August.

The artificial lakes of the Morvan, built in the nineteenth century to control the flow of the river Yonne and to create energy, now provide recreational areas in the Regional Park. Fish such as pike and zander from the lakes and trout from the streams is often eaten 'à la Morvandelle', although this appears to be interpreted in a variety of ways.

ABOVE The Lac de Pannesière, *through which flows the river Yonne. This is the largest man-made lake in the Morvan and the most attractive. A favourite haunt of fishermen, it is rich in pike and zander.*

TOP A peaceful view of the Cure river in the Morvan wilderness near Saint-André-en-Morvan, a village and landscape which inspired the nineteenth-century painter, Corot.

LEFT Dancers of the Morvan, wearing traditional costume, perform to the sound of the vielle, *a traditional instrument which is still made in Burgundy.*

ABOVE Pain de campagne, *one of the many types of country loaves sold by bakeries in response to an increasing demand for whole wheat and natural yeast.*

BELOW Crayfish, once abundant in Morvan streams, have almost disappeared and may be fished for only one week a year.

PIGEONS

*Traditional dovecotes lend grace to the
countryside of Burgundy but most no longer
serve their original purpose.
Nowadays domestic pigeons tend to be kept in
purpose-built cages. Tucked away at the end of
the tiny village of Athée is the house
of the Lehujeur family. Some distance from the
house is a large building which contains
a row of wire-mesh cages, home to a flock of
silvery grey and white pigeons.
Apart from the Lehujeurs, there are only
two professional pigeon breeders in Burgundy.
The Lehujeurs started breeding pigeons in
partnership with the Delomaz family in 1987
when they left Paris for the Morvan.
The young pigeons, or squabs, should
be eaten when they are about twenty-eight days
old before they start to fly. Most varieties of
pigeon bred in France seem to come
from America because the imported birds are
more resistant to disease and have a
better flavour. In addition to selling oven-ready
birds, the Lehujeurs also prepare and
bottle terrines, pigeon foie gras, pigeon rillettes
and pigeons confits. These can be bought
at the markets of Avallon and Saulieu from
the Delomaz stall.*

THE FORESTS

Mushrooms are an abiding concern for the people of the Morvan. Three hundred different species grow in the area and, as soon as the local woodcutter announces that he has found the first mushrooms of the season, the rest of the village joins in the fun of the search. Individuals pride themselves on their ability to find wild mushrooms and there is a great sense of achievement in discovering large, firm brown ceps or the rare amethysts. Mushrooms are an important ingredient in local cooking. They are served either fresh or dried and are used in the winter in terrines. The abundance of the crop varies from year to year depending on moon cycles and the weather.

Hunting for mushrooms is a secretive affair as no one wants to alert others to the location of prize mushroom sites. However, competition is not only local: groups of outsiders known as 'Turks' gather mushrooms in the forest and sell them at Rungis market just outside Paris. The locals are outraged by this, many expressing the view that there should be a law against people stealing their mushrooms. So fierce is their sense of entitlement to the crop in their own area that one can provoke the rage of one's whole village by betraying the best location to an outsider.

The best season for mushrooms is the autumn, when collection points are set up throughout the Morvan. Pickers assemble at these points with their mushrooms which are then sorted and taken by truck to Paris where they appear on sale the following day.

*LEFT Mushrooms are found all year round in the Morvan but are most abundant in autumn. Local restaurants offer a wide selection of dishes for the mushroom lover. The species pictured here are, from top left, girolles, amethyst or pied bleu, pied de mouton and pleurote de souche.
Below, from left to right, are trompettes de la mort, cèpes des pins and chanterelles en tube. These examples were exhibited at the annual mushroom fair at the Auberge de l'Atre, outside Quarré-les-Tombes.*

Numerous varieties are sold in the local markets of the Morvan: the very rare Caesar, the large, brown, bulbous ceps or the prized morels. As ceps mature they turn from white to yellow then green, so they have to be picked young and dried or eaten while still white.

In the past, whenever they were available, mushrooms formed the basis of soup, which was a staple dish of the Morvandiaux. These soups were simple, often made with a handful of vegetables, dried beans and a little bacon and then poured over grilled *pain de campagne*. A highly refined version of this is the cep soup with marjoram (see page 54).

Another foodstuff traditionally gleaned from the forest was chestnuts. They were made into a gruel, roasted on the fire or simmered with vegetables and bacon (see recipe on page 56); sometimes they were mixed with chocolate to make a dessert. Chestnut flour was used to make bread when wheat or other grain was unavailable. On the last Sunday in October a chestnut market is held in the village of Saint-Léger-sous-Beuvray near Autun.

ABOVE Bicycles mark a cycle trail in the Morvan Regional Park, which has encouraged the development of sporting activities such as horseriding and hiking, windsurfing on the lakes, and fishing, canoeing and white-water rafting in the rivers. RIGHT Dense pine forests line the river Canches.

FARMING IN THE MORVAN

Gérard Maternaud and his wife are native Morvandiaux from near Quarré-les-Tombes. Their farm lies at the end of a dirt track in the woods around Quarré. A Charolais cattle breeder until he was put out of business by a competitor, in 1969 Gérard started growing strawberries. By 1982 he was producing enough vegetables to supply most of the restaurants of the region, and now he also grows pine trees for Christmas. His sons and daughter all work in the business. Gérard is a short, thickset man with a Morvandiau drawl. As we talked in his kitchen, Madame Maternaud was preparing a *jardinière* with fresh peas and ham for Sunday lunch for about fifteen people – her own family and the farmworkers who eat with them every day. Monsieur Maternaud sends mini-vegetables to Ireland (popular with restaurants for their visual appeal) and mushrooms as far as Japan. He grows fifty kinds of vegetable and most of the seeds come from England: round carrots, parsnips (a neglected vegetable in France which is now being reintroduced), salad beet, root parsley, and a wide variety of common herbs as well as ruffle (purple basil), chervil, anis, *musc de provence*, purslane, lovage and savory. His farming is organic and he uses about three hundred tonnes of manure a year, most of which comes from organic farms.

TOP AND ABOVE Gérard Maternaud farms land in the middle of the Morvan forest, growing a variety of vegetables and fruit for local markets and restaurants. Strawberries, raspberries and redcurrants are a large part of his production
RIGHT A small herd of Charolais cattle being driven along a narrow lane near Saulieu. Cattle are bred in the Morvan but, because of the poor pastures, are usually sold when young at the livestock markets of Moulins-Engelbert or Saint-Christophe-en-Brionnais (see pages 99-101).

MORVAN HAMS

The best hams are the ones prepared by *charcutiers* from local pigs – a cross between the Charolais and Yorkshire breeds. These pigs roam almost wild in the forests of the Morvan and are said to have a special flavour. The hams are never smoked; instead they are rubbed with salt, pepper, garlic and vinegar and kept in a cool salt house for thirty days. They are then hung in loose cotton for at least six months to dry in well-ventilated rooms; in the past most Morvan houses had hams hanging from the rafters.

Hams can be bought whole or in slices. Some *charcutiers* debone them and sell them vacuum-packed. A light snack called *grèle* consists of a slice of ham cooked over an open fire and eaten on bread much like an open sandwich.

Having trained at the large ham factory of Dussert in Arleuf, Micheline Gaudry opened a charcuterie in Château-Chinon in 1957 with her Lyonnais husband. Her shop is open all day every day, and Madame Gaudry starts work at around four in the morning with the baking of *gougères*, *brioche-aux-griaudes* and duck pâtés. Winter activites include the preparation of ham, smoked bacon, *saucisson cendré*, *rosette*, *judru* (all local dry sausages), salt pork and *andouilles* (sausages made from the intestines of the pig). Most sausages are prepared

ABOVE LEFT Hams of the Morvan are air dried in stiff gauze bags suspended from rafters.
ABOVE RIGHT A charcuterie in Château-Chinon with an attractive early-twentieth-century frontage.
Most charcuteries in Corbigny and Lormes still prepare local specialities.

BRIOCHES AND GALETTES

Brioches-aux-griaudes and galettes-aux-griaudes are found in charcuteries throughout most of Burgundy. Griaudes are the pieces of pork crackling which remain after the lard (saindoux) has been melted from the meat. The lard is sold in attractive little white conical mounds for use in cooking, although this practice is fast disappearing.

The griaudes are incorporated into the dough and the resulting brioche or galette is eaten as a snack or with salad. Galettes are made with bread dough and shaped like a round pizza while brioches are made with a sweeter dough and shaped like a filled crown.

In La Clayette prunes are incorporated into the brioche while in Chalon and Autun pink praslines (sugar-coated almonds) are added to the dough.

ABOVE Andouilles *in brine at the Charcuterie Gaudry in Château-Chinon.*
BELOW *This attractive sign outside the delicatessen of Yves Perreau in Saulieu offers an enticement to enter one of the finest shops in the region.*

in November when the weather is cool and the meat will not spoil. The sausages will then be sold in June and July once the drying process is complete.

Each pig yields four *andouilles* and a Morvan speciality consists of a large *andouille* cooked with white haricot beans. *Andouilles* are also cooked in white wine, as in Chablis. Considered a delicacy in France, there is a great demand for *andouilles*, and some Morvan butchers send them as far as Paris. The intestines are cut into strips, seasoned with pepper, garlic, vinegar and salt, then marinated for a month.

On the main shopping street of Saulieu, tucked in between a line of bakeries and an old-fashioned café complete with a wooden bar and 1920s mirrors, stands the shop of Perrau, a charcutier and *traiteur*. The shop makes a local speciality, *Tourte Morvandelle*, a covered puff pastry pie with pork marinated in white wine, similar to the *Tourte Bourguignonne* (see recipe on page 36). Potatoes were often added to this pie and, in some places, such as Lormes and Corbigny, the pie used to be made either of potatoes or of pork.

HONEY

Among other escapees from city life who are keen to help regenerate the Morvan and create profitable businesses are Dominique and Jean-Jacques Coppin, a young couple who have settled outside Château-Chinon. Dominique, president of the Association d'Artistes Producteurs et Artisans du Morvan, organizes the picking and sorting of local mushrooms and is an ardent defender of the produce and customs of the Morvan. The Coppins started to produce honey in 1976 and they have been winning gold and silver medals at agricultural fairs ever since.

Their eight hundred beehives are distributed throughout the Morvan and yield between five hundred kilos and one tonne a day during the honey season – which runs from May to August – making an average of twenty-five to fifty tonnes of honey a year. Jean-Jacques places the hives near plants with which he wishes to flavour the honey, but although bees usually opt for the closest species they cannot be relied upon to do so. The harvest is unpredictable in quantity, quality and type. This is partially a result of weather conditions, which affect not only the activities of the bees, but also the flowers from which the bees draw nectar. Jean-Jacques' eyes flashed with amusement as he described the bees returning heavily laden with pollen to the hives, barely managing to fly, as if drunk. Like wine, honey has a different flavour each year and some years are better than others.

The honey is neither treated nor heated in any way. The amber liquid is sealed in combs on man-made wooden trays which slide in and out of the hive. The honey is extracted by centrifuge, filtered twice, then allowed to rest for between two weeks and a month; it must not be allowed to age for too long or it will lose its taste and all its nutrients. Faithful customers wait for the Coppins' honey to be ready each year before making special trips to Château-Chinon to buy it. Besides pine, chestnut, wild flower and acacia honey, the Coppins make a dark, golden, moist *pain d'épices* full of honey. They also manufacture beeswax candles and polish.

ABOVE AND RIGHT Beehives outside Château-Chinon, tended by their owner, Jean-Jacques Coppin. Different types of honey can be sampled at the Coppin family shop. BELOW Beeswax moulds for sale.

JAM MAKING AT TRINQUELIN

Burgundy is famous for jams such as raisiné *(made from grapes) or* épine-vinette *(made from rose-hips). Most patisseries and even some of the great restaurants such as the Vieux Moulin, near Beaune, sell home-made jams. A few professionals, like Bernard Bérilley, a native of Trinquelin, make jam the whole year round. I found this slim, bearded man in his workroom, stirring raspberry jam in a large copper basin with a long wooden paddle. His cooling device comprises a supermarket trolley, suspended by chains and lowered, with the jams, into cold water. He makes a variety of jams using only the best fruit and the minimum of sugar, which means that they are thinner than usual and very tangy. Among the twenty-two varieties of jam he produces are apricot, redcurrant, quince and elderflower. In 1982 he made two thousand pots using only his own fruit. His production has now increased to seventy thousand pots a year. His cherry jam is made from a cherry called Belle de Juillet, supplied by a producer near Coulanges-la-Vineuse who continues to grow them especially for him.*

ABOVE AND BELOW At Villapourçon Luc Digonnet and his family make crottins *and a large, creamy Tomme du Morvan from goats' milk .*

ABOVE A Tomme, a new cheese from the Abbaye de la Pierre-qui-Vire, is left in farmhouse cellars for several months to mature.
LEFT AND BELOW The first stage of draining the cows' milk cheese, after the addition of rennet. The cheese is then turned over, displaying the distinctive holes made by the draining receptacle. It is then salted on both sides before being left to dry (below).

ABOVE La Boule des Moines, a fresh cheese mixed with herbs and garlic, is produced at the farmhouse of the Abbaye de la Pierre-qui-Vire.
LEFT AND TOP Market stalls in Saulieu offer inviting arrays of goats' cheeses at different stages of maturation.

*ABOVE AND BELOW On a farm in an idyllic valley
near Onlay, farmer François Guyonnet has
started making ewes' milk cheeses.*

GOATS' CHEESE

Another producer who has settled in the Morvan is Luc Digonnet who makes goats' cheese in the hills outside the town of Villapourçon. Luc is an outgoing, thoughtful man who decided to leave the bustle of city life for the more peaceful surroundings of the Morvan. He explained to me that cheese-making is a delicate business and that cheese must be treated *'comme une jeune mariée, il ne fallait pas la bousculer'* (like a bride, it should not be rushed).

The president of Fromages Caprins de Bourgogne, which represents makers of goats' cheese in Burgundy, he has a herd of one hundred white Saanen goats, whose milk he uses to make a new cheese, Tomme du Morvan. This large, creamy cheese with a delicate, pungent taste, matured to the finest and most supple of textures, was created to diversify from the usual *crottins*, which remain the most popular with his customers.

ABBEY CHEESES

There are few foods as delicious as the fresh white cheese produced from the pastures of the Morvan. In the north-east corner of the region, approached by roads that are framed by tall trees, charming in summer but foreboding on dark, winter days, stands the Benedictine Abbaye de la Pierre-qui-Vire. (Built in the second half of the nineteenth century, it takes its name from a granite dolmen which was said to move, though if it ever did move, it does so no longer as it has been cemented down.) Despite the imposing size of the monastery, only seventy-five monks live there. The abbey owns sixty hectares of pasture, ten of cereals and fifty of woodland, and until 1988 the land was farmed by the monks themselves. From 1938 they made the Pierre-qui-Vire cheeses for which the abbey is famous. In 1969 the monks adopted organic breeding and cheese-making methods.

Since 1988, however, the abbey farm has been let to a Norman couple, the Anthores, because the abbot felt that the monks' farm duties interfered with their religious devotions. The Anthores continue to make the cheeses which are as popular as ever. They are served in the dining halls and sold in the monastery shop.

The Anthores are now on the brink of retirement but their young daughter, Elizabeth, is taking over, full of both hope and trepidation as she embarks on a number of changes: the whole dairy is being rebuilt according to EU standards.

A herd of forty Alpine Brown cattle produce the milk for a variety of cheeses made on the farm: a traditional fromage frais – sold in the old manner (*moulé à la louche*, meaning scooped up with a soup ladle and rather than being whisked); a *boule* of Pierre-qui-Vire, a fresh cream cheese with garlic and herbs, and a new cheese, a type of *tomme*, reminiscent of Cantal, from the Auvergne. When Elizabeth was explaining how their cheeses were made her mother interjected, warning her not to give away all the details. She laughed and said she had omitted vital steps. I reminded them that making good cheese was difficult and could not be learnt from one recipe in a book.

LA COTE D'OR

2, RUE ARGENTINE, 21210 SAULIEU, TEL 80 64 07 66

The construction of the autoroute to the south now bypasses Saulieu and, consequently, had put a stop to the obligatory en route *lunch at La Côte d'Or. However, innovative chef Bernard Loiseau has helped to put Saulieu back on the map. He started working at the restaurant in 1975, and bought the establishment in 1983. Numerous prizes attest to his talent; in 1995 Bernard Loiseau was awarded the Légion d'Honneur by President Mitterand for his services to France. The only other French chef to have received this award in the last twenty years is Paul Bocuse. Now Parisians take the fast train, the* Train à Grand Vitesse, *just to have lunch or dinner with one of the new leaders of Burgundian cuisine.*

Bernard Loiseau reinvents the great traditional dishes of the region, taking care not to use anything but natural and simple flavours, little or no fat, little sugar and the best possible produce, fresh and flavourful. This type of cooking is called 'la cuisine du jus' and, indeed, relies on the natural juices of the ingredients to make a dish succulent.

LA POULARDE
A LA VAPEUR
'ALEXANDRE DUMAINE'

Steamed Bresse Hen with Truffles

Alexandre Dumaine, former chef of the Côte d'Or, has influenced many of today's great chefs. This is one of his signature dishes, here adapted by Bernard Loiseau.

SERVES 4
1.8-1.9 kg/4-4¼ lb Bresse hen or good
quality free-range chicken
3tbsp brandy
3tbsp Madeira
150ml/5fl oz truffle juice
30g/1oz bottled truffles
1 small leek, cut into matchsticks
1 small carrot, cut into matchsticks
1 small turnip, cut into matchsticks
30g/1oz chicken livers
2l/3 ½ pt chicken stock
1.5l/2 ½ pt oxtail stock

125g/4½oz basmati rice
150g/5½oz butter
salt and freshly ground black pepper

One day ahead, prepare the marinade. Heat the brandy and Madeira in a saucepan, then set alight. When the flames die down, add 3 tablespoons of the truffle juice. Leave to cool.

Slice 4 thin rounds of truffle. Place a slice under the skin of each breast and thigh. Steam the leek, carrot and turnip together over boiling water for 4-5 minutes. Sauté the livers for 4 minutes in a small frying pan until browned, then cut them into small pieces.

Rinse the chicken inside and out, then dry it with paper towels. Mix the vegetables with the chicken livers, then stuff the chicken with the mixture. Place in a shallow oven-proof dish, pour over the marinade and chill overnight.

The next day, pour the stocks into a flame-proof earthenware casserole large enough to accommodate the dish containing the chicken. Place a ceramic stand in the bottom and then the dish with the chicken in the marinade on top. Season the chicken. Cover the casserole with the lid and then a damp tea towel.

Place the casserole over a very low heat to prevent the chicken becoming tough during cooking. Once the lid is very hot, cook the chicken for 1¼ hours, pouring tepid water over the lid 3 or 4 times. Remove from the heat and let the chicken rest for 10 minutes.

Meanwhile, cook the rice, drain and return it to the saucepan. Finely chop the rest of the truffles and stir into the rice along with the truffle juice and butter over a low heat.

Take the lid off the casserole and pour 2 ladles of the cooking stock over the chicken.

Cut the chicken into serving pieces. Place each piece on a plate with rice and stuffing. Pour a few ladlefuls of cooking stock over the chicken pieces and stuffing.

LA ROSE DES SABLES

Desert Roses (Illustrated above)

SERVES 4
FOR THE ORANGE SAUCE
3 oranges plus juice of 6 oranges
2kg/4½lb sugar

FOR THE BISCUITS
6 egg whites
140g/5oz icing sugar, sifted
75g/2½oz plain flour, sifted
75g/2½oz clarified butter, melted
30g/1oz cocoa powder, sifted

FOR THE SORBET
500ml/16fl oz milk
450g/1lb sugar
200g/7oz cocoa powder, sifted
150g/5½oz good quality dark chocolate

Prepare the sauce a day ahead. Make a cut in each orange and blanch in boiling water. Put 3l/5¼pt water and the sugar in a saucepan and bring to the boil. Stir to dissolve the sugar before the water boils. Add the oranges and simmer gently, covered, for 6 hours, skimming the surface. Drain and purée the oranges. Stir in the orange juice, leave to cool, then cover with cling film and refrigerate.

Preheat the oven to 180°C/350°F/gas mark 4.

For the biscuits, beat the egg whites until soft peaks form, add the sugar and beat until stiff. Fold in the flour, butter and cocoa powder. Place twenty 8cm/3¼in rounds of the mixture on a chilled baking sheet. Bake for 3 minutes until just golden around the edges. Leave to set for 2 minutes, then transfer to a wire rack to cool.

Put all the sorbet ingredients in a saucepan with 1l/1¾pts of water and heat to dissolve the sugar and melt the chocolate. Bring to the boil, then leave to cool before placing in an ice-cream maker for 15 minutes. Alternatively, follow the directions for the sorbet on page 91.

Pour the sauce around 4 plates, then make a tower with 5 biscuits and 4 sorbet scoops.

L'AUBERGE DE L'ATRE

LES LAVAULTS, 89630 QUARRE-LES-TOMBES, TEL 86 32 20 79

In a clearing in the woods lining the road outside Quarré-les-Tombes lies L'Auberge de L'Atre (the Inn of the Hearth), run by Francis and Odile Salamolard. Inspired by the wilderness of the Morvan, Francis Salamolard adopted the district after spending years abroad. The friendly, unpretentious atmosphere in this quiet Morvan farm makes an overnight stay a must. Using local produce and wines from the Yonne (Chablis, Irancy, Epineuil and Coulanges) he offers, for a very reasonable price, a small but select choice of, for instance, scallops with Chablis and mustard duck with rosemary. When autumn comes and the hunting season starts, venison, hare, pheasant and partridge appear on the menu.

SOMMELIER LYONEL LECONTE

The Burgundian love of wine exists even in the Morvan. Lyonel Leconte, the twenty-nine-year-old sommelier (wine steward) at La Côte d'Or recently won the award for the best sommelier in France.

This enthusiastic young man, who became chef sommelier at La Côte d'Or at the age of twenty-five, believes, as does Loiseau, that the role of a restaurant and of a sommelier is to bring a little happiness into the lives of the guests.

The wine list at La Côte d'Or has five hundred and eighty-eight different wines, ranging from prestige labels to more modestly priced bottles; it includes one hundred and twenty-two white and one hundred and seventy-nine red Burgundy wines.

The selection of wines is carried out throughout the year and involves visits to vineyards two or three times a week. Leconte, Loiseau and Hubert Couillaud, director of the restaurant, taste first from the barrels and then again with the other sommeliers. Leconte's forté is finding the perfect complement to each dish, and he surprises even connoisseurs with his excellent recommendations.

CUISSOT D'AGNEAU AUX LARDONS

Leg of Lamb with Lardons

The lamb here is roasted in the same way as venison, hence the use of 'cuissot' meaning haunch of venison. (Illustrated opposite)

SERVES 4-6
750ml/27fl oz white Burgundy wine
1tbsp brandy
1 onion, chopped
2 carrots, sliced
1 sprig fresh thyme
2 sprigs fresh flat-leaf parsley
1 bay leaf
12.5kg/5 ½ lb leg of lamb
100g/3 ½ oz smoked streaky back bacon, rinded and cut into lardons
100g/3 ½ oz unsalted butter, diced
salt and freshly ground black pepper

The day before mix the wine, brandy, onion, carrots and herbs together in a large non-metallic bowl. Add the lamb, cover and chill for 24 hours. Turn the leg over occasionally.

Preheat the oven to 250°C/475°F/gas mark 8.

The next day, remove the lamb from the marinade and let it come to room temperature. Drain the herbs and vegetables from the marinade, reserving the liquid, and transfer them to a roasting tin. Cut slits in the lamb and insert the lardons. Season and place on top of the vegetables. Roast for 1 hour and 5 minutes until well done on the outside and slightly pink in the centre. Remove the lamb from the tin, cover with foil and leave for 20 minutes.

Pour the reserved liquid into the tin, bring to the boil and simmer for 5 minutes. Whisk in the butter, season and serve with the lamb.

CHARLOTTE AU CHOCOLAT ET AUX NOISETTES

Chocolate and Hazelnut Charlotte

(Illustrated above)

SERVES 6
55g/2oz butter
250g/8 ½ oz best-quality dark chocolate
175g/6½ oz hazelnut praline
6 eggs, separated
24 sponge fingers
55g/2oz sugar
90ml/3fl oz cherry *eau de vie*

Melt the butter, chocolate and praline in a bowl standing over a pan of simmering water.

Remove the bowl from the heat and beat in the egg yolks, then leave the chocolate mixture to cool to room temperature.

Arrange the sponge fingers evenly on a deep plate. Mix the sugar, *eau de vie* and 100ml/3 ½ fl oz of water together and sprinkle over the sponge fingers. Line a 1.5l/2½ pt charlotte mould or a loaf tin with the fingers, placing them in rows along the bottom, then standing them up along the sides.

Whisk the egg whites until stiff, then fold into the chocolate mixture. Pour the mixture into the mould. Trim the fingers so that they are level with the chocolate. Cover with cling film and chill for at least 6 hours.

Turn out the mould by holding a serving plate over the top and then inverting it with a sharp shake. Remove the mould. Serve with custard sauce or vanilla ice-cream.

CRAPIAUX DU MORVAN

Morvan Crêpes

Crapiaux are said to be the 'male' of the crêpe, in other words a thick, solid affair. They can be made with buckwheat or potatoes.

SERVES 4
FOR BUCKWHEAT CREPES
200g/7oz buckwheat flour
pinch of salt
2 eggs, lightly beaten
85ml/3fl oz crème fraîche
6 lean bacon rashers, rinded and halved
1tsp butter, for frying

Preheat the grill to high. Sift the flour and salt into a bowl and make a well in the centre. Add the eggs to the well and gradually draw in some of the flour. Pour in 85ml/3fl oz of water and the crème fraîche, whisking to gradually incorporate the remaining flour until smooth. Set the batter aside for at least 30 minutes.

Meanwhile, grill the bacon until crisp.

Grease a small frying pan and heat over a high heat. Place one piece of bacon in the hot pan and pour over 2 tablespoons of batter. Fry each side until golden brown and drain on paper towels. Continue frying until all the batter is used. Butter the pan when necessary.

FOR POTATO CREPES
200g/7oz baking potatoes
45g/1½oz fromage frais
2tbsp plain flour
1 egg
1tsp butter, for frying
salt and freshly ground black pepper

Boil the potatoes in salted water until tender, then peel and mash with the fromage frais and

POTAGE DE POMMES DE TERRE AUX CEPES

Potato Soup with Ceps

If you cannot find fresh ceps, substitute with any other wild or button mushrooms, adding a handful of dried ceps to give more flavour. (Illustrated above)

SERVES 4
55g/2oz onions, finely chopped
whites of 2 leeks, finely chopped
1tbsp butter
750ml/27fl oz chicken or vegetable stock
150g/5½oz waxy potatoes, thinly sliced
200g/7oz fresh ceps, sliced
1tbsp olive oil
pinch of grated nutmeg
1tbsp chopped fresh chervil
1tbsp chopped fresh marjoram
2tbsp crème fraîche
salt and freshly ground black pepper

Sauté the onions and the leeks in the butter in a large saucepan until translucent. Add the stock and the potatoes and bring to the boil, then simmer for 20 minutes.

Meanwhile, sauté the ceps in a frying pan in the olive oil for 5 minutes. Remove the ceps from the pan and set aside.

When the potatoes are tender, season generously with salt, pepper and nutmeg, add the ceps, herbs and crème fraîche and simmer for 5 minutes over a gentle heat without letting the soup boil. Serve immediately.

the flour. When cool whisk in the egg. Season. Melt the butter in a large frying pan. When the butter is hot, drop in tablespoons of the potato mixture. Fry until golden on both sides.

CHORLATTE

Pumpkin and Mushroom Flan in Spinach Leaves

This used to be made by baking the filling slowly in cabbage leaves in the dying heat of a baker's oven. The custard was thickened with flour. You can either leave the pumpkin in chunks or you can purée it. (Illustrated right)

SERVES 4
150ml/5fl oz single cream
pinch of grated nutmeg
6 sprigs fresh chervil, finely chopped
3 eggs
350g/12oz pumpkin, cooked and puréed
15 large spinach leaves
115g/4oz button mushrooms or ceps, sliced
30g/1oz butter, plus extra for greasing
salt and freshly ground pepper

Preheat the oven to 180°C/350°F/gas mark 4. Grease a round 575ml/1pt soufflé dish. Whisk the cream, nutmeg, chervil, eggs and seasoning together. Whisk in the pumpkin purée.

Carefully dip the spinach leaves, one by one, in boiling water for a few seconds. Arrange the leaves overlapping in the dish. Pat the leaves dry with paper towels if necessary.

Sauté the mushrooms in the butter. Fold into the pumpkin, then pour into the dish.

Bake in the middle of the oven for 45 minutes or until a knife inserted into the centre comes out clean. Leave to set for a few minutes. Unmould and serve warm.

BLETTES AUX LARDONS

Spinach Beet with Bacon

SERVES 4
1kg/2 ¼ lb spinach beet or Swiss chard
small bunch sorrel
butter, for greasing

FOR THE CREAM SAUCE
1tbsp butter
1tbsp plain flour
250ml/8fl oz vegetable stock or water
100ml/3 ½ fl oz single cream
2 egg yolks, lightly beaten
100g/3½ oz streaky bacon, cut into lardons
pinch of grated nutmeg
salt and freshly ground black pepper

Melt the butter in a saucepan. Stir in the flour over a medium heat until the mixture bubbles. Pour in the stock and bring to the boil, whisking. Simmer, uncovered, over a low heat for 20 minutes. Whisk in two-thirds of the cream. Bring to the boil, then remove from the heat. Beat the egg yolks into the rest of the cream. Whisk this mixture into the saucepan, then add the nutmeg and seasoning.

Sauté the lardons in a dry frying pan until crisp, then leave to drain on paper towels.

Preheat the oven to 180°C/350°F/gas mark 4. Lightly butter a gratin dish. Pull the beet leaves from the stalks and reserve. Cut off any strings from the stalks and slice thickly. Boil the slices for 10 minutes in salted water, then drain and refresh under cold water. Cook the beet leaves and sorrel in a pan, without any water, for 1-2 minutes until wilted. Stir into the sauce.

Layer the stalks in the dish. Sprinkle with half the lardons and half the sauce. Sprinkle over the rest of the lardons and finish with the sauce. Bake for 30 minutes or until browned.

CHATAIGNES AU LARD

Chestnuts with Bacon

SERVES 4
800g/1 ¾ lb whole chestnuts
2tsp sunflower oil
225g/8 ½ oz lean bacon, rind removed
55g/2oz lard
1 celery stalk, sliced
1 sprig of fresh thyme
½ tsp sugar
800ml/28fl oz chicken or vegetable stock
salt and freshly ground black pepper

Preheat the oven to 180°C/350°F/gas mark 4.

Cut a cross on the flat side of each chestnut. Place them in a roasting tin, coat with the oil and cook over a high heat for about 10 minutes until the skins peel away easily.

Blanch the bacon, then drain, dice it and Place the bacon and peeled chestnuts in a flame-proof casserole. Add the remaining ingredients and season. Simmer, covered, for 30 minutes until the chestnuts are tender. Serve with venison or roast pork.

CARPE A LA MORVANDELLE

Carp Stuffed with Choux Pastry

This is an old-fashioned way of preparing carp, which is now more often sold in fillets and cooked in red wine with lardons. You can use bream if you cannot find carp.

SERVES 4-6
half the quantity of choux pastry dough
(see recipe on page 30), omitting the cheese
1.35kg/3lb carp, scaled and cleaned

200ml/7fl oz dry white wine
100ml/3½ fl oz marc or Madeira
85g/3oz butter
30g/1oz breadcrumbs
salt and freshly ground black pepper
small bunch flat-leaf parsley, finely
chopped, to garnish

Preheat the oven to 180°C/350°F/gas mark 4.

Fill the central cavity of the carp with the choux pastry dough, reserving about 3 tablespoons. Sew up the cavity using a trussing needle and cotton thread. Place the fish in a roasting pan with the wine and marc. Season with salt and freshly ground black pepper, dot with butter and sprinkle with the breadcrumbs. Bake in the oven for 35 minutes or until the flesh flakes easily when tested with the tip of a knife.

Just before serving, drop teaspoons of the reserved pastry dough into a saucepan of boiling water and poach for 5 minutes.

Remove the thread from the carp and transfer to a serving dish. Sprinkle each portion with the parsley and serve with the choux pastry stuffing and the poached pastry.

SANDRE A L'OSEILLE

Zander Stuffed with Sorrel

SERVES 4
1.35kg/3lb zander, cleaned
575ml/1pt white Burgundy wine

FOR THE STUFFING
250g/½ lb each fresh sorrel and spinach
1tbsp butter
3 shallots, finely chopped
55g/2oz fresh white breadcrumbs
salt and freshly ground black pepper

FOR THE SAUCE
1 shallot, finely chopped
1tbsp butter
575ml/1pt crème fraîche
225g/8oz fresh sorrel or spinach, chopped

Preheat the oven to 200°C/400°F/gas mark 6.

For the stuffing, rinse the sorrel and spinach leaves in cold water. Remove the stalks from the sorrel and the central veins from the spinach.

Melt the butter in a saucepan, add the shallots and sauté for 3-4 minutes, stirring. Add the rinsed leaves and sauté for 3-4 minutes. Squeeze out the excess moisture using the back of a spoon, then stir in the breadcrumbs. Season with salt and freshly ground black pepper. Stuff the central cavity of the fish with the stuffing mixture.

Place the fish in a baking tin, pour in the wine, cover with a lid or kitchen foil and poach for 30 minutes until the flesh flakes easily. Transfer to a serving platter and keep warm. Reserve the poaching liquid.

To make the sauce, sauté the shallot in the butter for 3-4 minutes. Add the reserved liquid and crème fraîche. Bring to the boil and then simmer for 20 minutes or until reduced and thick. Stir in the chopped sorrel or spinach and cook for a few minutes until tender. Pour the sauce over the fish and serve at once.

PIGEONNEAUX DU MORVAN AUX CERISES

Pigeons with Cherries

Pigeons are a common sight on any restaurant menu in Burgundy. They can be cooked with honey and spices or with petit pois.

SERVES 4
115g/4oz butter
4 oven-ready, young pigeons
8 bacon rashers
1tbsp vegetable oil
2 carrots, finely chopped
2 onions, finely chopped
2 garlic cloves, crushed
57ml/5tbsp wine vinegar
250ml/8fl oz chicken stock
350g/12oz cherries, stoned
1tbsp honey
salt and freshly ground black pepper

Preheat the oven to 230°C/450°F/gas mark 8.

Season the birds inside and out. Wrap the rashers round the breasts, securing them with string or wooden cocktail sticks. Place in a roasting tin with the vegetables and cover with 30g/1oz of melted butter and the oil. Roast for 30 minutes, turning the birds over once.

Remove the pigeons from the tin, cover with foil and set aside. Drain the fat from the tin, then de-glaze the tin with the vinegar over a medium heat, scraping the base. Add the stock and simmer for 5 minutes, stirring from time to time. Pour the sauce through a sieve into a saucepan, add the cherries and honey and simmer for 5 minutes, stirring occasionally.

Place the pigeons on a warmed serving plate, surrounded by the cherries. Whisk the remaining butter into the sauce. Spoon the sauce over the pigeons and serve at once.

POULET A LA MORVANDELLE

Chicken with Morvan Ham, Onions and Potatoes

This delicious chicken dish is simple to cook. Use Parma ham or any other dry-cured ham if you cannot find the regional speciality.

SERVES 4
1.35-1.5 kg/3-3 ½ lb free-range chicken
85g/3oz butter
20 pickling onions or 5 medium onions
20 small waxy potatoes, peeled
200g/7oz dry cured ham, roughly chopped
large bunch flat-leaf parsley, finely chopped
juice of ½ lemon
salt and freshly ground black pepper

Preheat the oven to 150°C/300°F/gas mark 2.

Season the chicken inside and out. In a flame-proof casserole, brown the chicken in half the butter. Transfer the chicken to an oven-proof dish and place in the oven.

Discard the fat from the casserole, then melt the rest of the butter in the casserole and sauté the onions and ham. Turn down the heat, cover and simmer for 10 minutes.

Return the chicken to the casserole. Turn up the oven to 200°C/400°F/gas mark 6. Add the potatoes, onions, ham and half the parsley to the casserole. Season, taking care not to over-salt because of the salt in the ham.

Cover and cook in the oven for 1 hour and 15 minutes or until the chicken is tender and the juices run clear if the thigh is pierced with the tip of a knife. Cut up the chicken and place on a serving dish, spooning over the cooking juices. Sprinkle with lemon juice and the remaining parsley and serve surrounded by the onion, potato and ham mixture.

POTEE BOURGUIGNONNE

Salt Pork with Bacon, Sausages and Mixed Vegetables

This is a feast dish, similar to the bouilli de Saint-Christophe, *and prepared according to each family's tradition. A* bouilli *is a common name for a plate of boiled meat.*

SERVES 6-8
1.5kg/3 ½ lb salt pork including a
small piece each of blade bone, spare ribs,
shinbone or hock and lean bacon
100g/3 ½ oz dried white haricot beans
heart of a small Savoy cabbage, quartered
and cored
1tbsp white wine vinegar
1 onion studded with 1 clove
1 celery stalk
2 sprigs of fresh thyme
1 bay leaf
4 sprigs of fresh parsley
200g/7oz carrots, peeled
3 leeks, white parts only
12 small pork sausages
2 small turnips, peeled
450g/1lb small, waxy potatoes, peeled
salt and freshly ground black pepper
Dijon mustard, to serve
gherkins, to serve
6 slices *pain de campagne*, to serve

The day before cooking place the beans in water to soak. The next day drain the beans, put them in a saucepan, cover with water and boil for 10 minutes, then simmer for 1 hour

Place all the pork in a large flame-proof casserole, cover with cold water and bring slowly to the boil. Drain and repeat, then boil for a further 10 minutes.

Wash the cabbage in water mixed with the vinegar. Put in a saucepan, cover with water and bring to the boil. Drain and refresh.

Add the onion, celery and herbs to the casserole. Cover with water and bring to the boil. Simmer for 40 minutes, uncovered, skimming off the scum. Add the carrots and beans and cook for 20 minutes.

Add the leeks and sausages. Simmer for 10 minutes. Add the cabbage, turnips and potatoes and simmer for a further 10 minutes. Season.

Serve the meat and vegetables on a platter with mustard and gherkins and the broth separately in a bowl with *pain de campagne*.

SAUPIQUET DES AMOGNES

Morvan Ham with Juniper and White Wine Sauce

Saupiquet is a term used to mean both sharp and salty. In this recipe, from the Amognes, the sharpness comes from the vinegar. Add only a small quantity of vinegar at a time until you achieve a sharpness to your taste.

Saupiquet was traditionally served with chestnuts – the sweetish taste of the chestnuts contrasts pleasantly with the ham sauce. (Illustrated right)

SERVES 4
8 slices of Morvan or Parma ham
milk, to cover ham
3tbsp butter
2tbsp plain flour
200ml/7fl oz dry white wine
2 shallots, finely chopped
100ml/3½ fl oz white wine vinegar
5 dried juniper berries, crushed
100ml/3½ fl oz single cream

small bunch parsley, finely chopped
3-4 sprigs fresh tarragon, finely chopped
salt and freshly ground black pepper

Place the ham in a dish, pour in enough milk to cover and leave for about 2 hours in a cool place. This will remove some of the saltiness.

Melt 2 tablespoons of the butter in a saucepan, then stir in the flour and cook for a few minutes over a low heat until slightly browned. Whisk in the wine, remove from the heat and set aside.

Put the shallots in a saucepan with the vinegar, juniper berries, salt and pepper and cook over a high heat until the vinegar is reduced by half.

Drain the ham, discarding the milk and pat dry with paper towels. Melt the remaining butter in a frying pan and sauté the ham on both sides for 5 minutes.

Strain the shallots and juniper berries and reserve the vinegar. Add the berries and shallots to the wine sauce. Gradually pour the vinegar into the sauce, according to taste. Gently whisk in the cream, then season to taste. Place the ham in warmed individual dishes or an earthenware serving dish and pour the sauce over. Sprinkle with the herbs.

PATE AUX POIRES

Double-crust Pear Tart

Small wild pears called daguenelles *were traditionally used whole in this dish. You can use Conference pears or dessert apples instead. (Illustrated right)*

SERVES 6

1kg/2 ¼ lb pears, peeled, cored and sliced
2tbsp lemon juice
4tbsp *eau de vie*
3tbsp ground almonds
85g/3oz sugar
1tbsp plain flour
1 egg, lightly beaten, for glazing
1 egg yolk (optional)
150ml/5fl oz single cream (optional)
pinch of salt and pepper

FOR THE PATE BRISEE
300g/10 ½ oz plain flour, sifted
pinch of salt
1tbsp sugar
1 egg yolk
150g/5 ½ oz butter

The day before cooking, place the pears in a bowl, cover with lemon juice and *eau de vie* and leave overnight.

Four hours before serving, prepare the pâte brisée. Put the flour in a bowl and make a well in the centre. Add the salt, sugar, egg, butter and 55ml/2fl oz of water. Mix quickly with your fingertips and add up to 55ml/2fl oz more water, if needed, to absorb all the flour. The dough does not need to be smooth. Shape the dough into a ball, wrap in cling film and chill for at least 2 hours.

Two hours before serving, roll out two-thirds of the dough on a lightly floured surface to line a deep 20cm/8in tart tin with a removeable base. Transfer the dough to the tin and trim the edges with a knife. Reserve the trimmings for decoration.

Preheat the oven to 180°C/350°F/gas mark 4.

Drain the pears and place in a bowl with the almonds, sugar, flour, some salt and pepper. Gently toss the pears in the dry mixture, then pack them tightly into the tart tin. Roll out the rest of the dough and use to cover the tart, brushing the edges with the beaten egg to seal. If you wish, decorate with pastry cuttings shaped into leaves or pears, stuck on with a little of the egg. Brush the pastry lid with the remaining egg to glaze. Carefully make a hole in the centre of the lid and insert a pie funnel or a cylinder of foil.

Bake for 45 minutes, covering with foil if the pastry starts to brown too much. Remove from the oven and place the tin on a wire rack.

While the tart is still warm, whisk the egg yolk into the cream, then pour the mixture into the pie through the funnel. Remove the tart from the tin and serve warm.

TARTE A LA SEMOULE

Semolina Tart

This dish was traditionally served to children as part of 'le goûter' or tea-time. Vincenot, a Burgundian novelist, remembers that there was always pastry available in his mother's kitchen for quiches or tarts such as this one. Sometimes sultanas soaked in marc or brandy are incorporated, or the tart is served with raspberry, redcurrant or blackcurrant jelly.

SERVES 6
500ml/16fl oz milk
75g/2½oz sugar
3tbsp butter
pinch of salt
½ vanilla pod, split lengthways
75g/2½oz semolina
1tbsp lemon juice
2 eggs, lightly beaten

FOR THE PASTRY
125g/4½oz butter, softened
75g/2½oz sugar
pinch of salt
finely grated zest of 1 lemon
1 egg, lightly beaten
250g/8½oz plain flour

FOR THE DECORATION (OPTIONAL)
100g/3½oz sugar
3tbsp single cream
32 walnuts or pecans

To make the pastry, put the butter, sugar, salt and lemon zest in a bowl and cream together. Add the egg and mix together well. Gradually add the flour to this mixture and work together with the palm of your hand until all the flour is absorbed and the dough is blended. Wrap the dough in cling film and refrigerate for at least 1 hour.

For the decoration, put the sugar in a small saucepan with a few drops of water over a low heat and stir until the sugar becomes amber coloured. Take the pan off the heat and carefully stir in the cream, drop by drop. Stop adding cream when the mixture is still thick. Dip in a few walnuts at a time, then place them on a metal rack to cool and dry.

Preheat the oven to 200°C/400°C/gas mark 6.

Roll the dough out to line a 20cm/8in tart tin with a removable base. Trim the edges. Line with baking parchment or foil, cover with dried beans and bake blind for 15 minutes.

Meanwhile, make the filling Bring the milk to the boil in a saucepan, then stir in the sugar, butter, salt and vanilla pod. Return to the boil and whisk in the semolina. Cook over a low heat for 2-3 minutes, whisking constantly.

Remove from the heat. When cool, scrape the seeds from the vanilla pod into the mixture. Discard the pod. Add the lemon juice.

Beat the eggs into the mixture. Pour into the half-baked tart shell and return to the oven. Bake for 25-30 minutes or until golden on top.

Leave to cool on a wire rack for 10 minutes before unmoulding. Decorate with the walnuts and serve warm or at room temperature.

PAIN DU BUCHERON

Woodcutter's Bread

This sourdough bread was bread that was made to last in the days when it could not be baked or bought every day. The recipe may seem time-consuming as the steps take several days to complete, but it is actually quite quick to make once the ingredients have fermented. It is delicious with strong cheese or charcuterie.

MAKES 2 LOAVES
1 sachet (11g/1tbsp) dried yeast
590g/1lb 5oz rye flour
550g/1¼lb wholemeal flour
2tbsp each of pumpkin seeds, sunflower seeds and linseeds
1tbsp salt

To make the sourdough starter, put half the yeast and 5 tablespoons of tepid water in a bowl and mix to dissolve. Add 55g/2oz of the rye flour, mix together, then cover tightly with cling film and put in a warm place for 24 hours to ferment. The starter will then smell sour and have a fairly solid appearance.

Add an additional 115g/4oz of rye flour and 175ml/6fl oz of tepid water to the starter and leave in a warm place, covered, for 4 hours.

Add 250g/8oz of the rye flour to the starter and a quarter of the remaining yeast. Add a little water if the dough is very dry but make sure it remains stiff. Leave in a warm place, covered with a damp cloth, for 1-2 hours.

Mix in the remaining rye flour, 200g/7oz of wholemeal flour with 225ml/8fl oz of tepid water, then leave to ferment for 1-2 hours.

Add an additional 250ml/8fl oz of tepid water, the seeds, salt, remaining yeast and wholewheat flour. Knead for a few minutes.

Make two balls from the dough, place them on a greased baking sheet and leave to rise in a warm place for about 1 hour; do not leave until double in bulk as the dough will tend to fall back. Leave the loaves uncovered while they are rising for a crustier loaf. Preheat the oven to 220°C/425°F/gas mark 7.

Put a roasting tin of water on the bottom shelf of the oven, sprinkle the loaves with flour and bake for 30 minutes. Remove the tin of water and bake for a further 30 minutes or until the loaves sound hollow when tapped on the bottom. Allow to cool on a wire rack.

BELOW *Neat rows of vines stretching into the distance near Pommard, south of Beaune. The red wines produced here are among the best known Burgundy appellations in the world.*
RIGHT *Dusty bottles in the cellar of the Gerbet family in Vosne-Romanée. Cellars are important features of traditional houses in Burgundy, and were usually served by a separate entrance. The town of Beaune has a honeycomb of wine cellars beneath its streets.*

TOP *The cat and the beehive on this Dijon patisserie sign symbolize the temptation of sweetness.*
ABOVE *The gargoyles of the gothic-style church of Notre-Dame lean dramatically out over the street behind the ducal palace in Dijon.*
TOP RIGHT *The colourful tiled roofs of the Hospices de Beaune, built in gothic style in 1443 by Nicholas Rollin, Chancellor of the Duke of Burgundy. Endowed with vineyards in the Côte de Beaune, the Hospices now own fifty-seven hectares of* grand crus *and* premier crus.

LA COTE D'OR

The ridge which gives its name to the *département* of the Côte d'Or (the Golden Slope) borders the last area of elevated land overlooking the Saône. The eastern face is covered with vines which extend over the gentle slopes of the hillsides and surround the villages.

The old capital of the Burgundian dukes, Dijon is the largest city in the area. It is the historic and administrative capital, with medieval buildings and a number of fine mansions. To the south lie magnificent vineyards, to the north the lush green hills and forests of the Châtillonais. The vast plain around Dijon furnishes the city with agricultural produce, while the town itself has become famous for the production of vinegars, mustards, patisserie and confectionery. It is claimed that the finest *pain d'épices* in France is made here.

One of the best and most interesting places to buy Burgundian produce is in and around the market in Dijon. In the centre of the market square stand large nineteenth-century *halles* (covered markets), currently undergoing renovation. Within are a dazzling array of stalls selling cheeses, honey, pastries, poultry, fish and various types of meat and charcuterie. Surrounding the *halles* are stalls offering fresh produce: flowers, fruit and vegetables – plump cherries, tiny wild strawberries, pale apricots, raspberries and redcurrants, white asparagus from Ruffey and glistening white onions from Auxonne. Elegantly dressed Dijonnais vie with each other for the best produce and everyone is encouraged to touch and smell before buying. A large rotisserie offers hot glazed meat – chicken, rabbit, guinea fowl, duck and turkey.

In a side street shoppers queue at a small bakery, La Gerbe d'Or. One man in his sixties, wearing a fedora explains to the old woman behind him that, although he lives in another part of Dijon, he always comes here to buy the bread, because, he explains, it is the best in town. Inside, the young women sell an array of breads: organic, rye, mixed grain with wholemeal, *pain de campagne*, *ficelle*, baguettes and brioches, but also *gougères*, *conversations* and *Paris-Brest*. A dark, heavy rye bread dotted with raisins, similar to that sold at Lionel Poilâne's famous bakery in Paris, is sold by weight for an astronomical sum. I succumb to temptation, join the queue and then, clutching my purchases, head for the cheese shop, Porcheret. I notice nearby the premises of the exceptional Raymond Fiquet, who sells the best tripe and sausages in the market. His products (terrines, *pâtés en croûte*, smoked ham, dry-cured ham and *saucissons*) are all made using the finest ingredients and are simple, fresh and delicious.

PAIN D'EPICES

The origins of pain d'épices *date back to the Ancient Egyptians who ate sweets cooked with honey. A Chinese bread called 'mi-kong' in which honey was mixed with the dough before baking, may have been brought to the West by the Mongols in the thirteenth century. It was passed on in turn to the crusaders by the Arabs and a sweet called boichet, made with honey and flour was a favourite of Marguerite of Flanders in the fourteenth century. Nowadays it takes the form of a large brown loaf called* le pavé de santé *('the paving stone of health', so-called because of its shape). Dijon has been associated with* pain d'épices *since the nineteenth century. The writer M.F.K. Fisher, writing about Dijon in the 1920s, remembers the sweet smell of the* pain d'épices *wafting all over town from the factories. Now the only large confectioner left in Dijon is Mulot et Petitjean, a family business for over a century. The shop, situated on the place Bossuet, retains its original panelled walls and tiles and is a regular stop for tourists (right). The* pain d'épices *from Mulot et Petitjean is the best known in Burgundy but the recipe is a family secret. The main ingredients are honey, flour, aniseed and fruit peel or spices (see recipe on page 91).*

Around the market the shops are crowded and the cafés are full; by twelve o'clock most tables will be taken. Bistros such as the Dôme provide delicious simple dishes inspired by market produce. One of the best times to go to Dijon is at the beginning of November, during the Foire Gastronomique de Dijon, which was initiated by the mayor, Gaston-Gérard, in 1921. The best producers of food and wine from the region offer tasting sessions and chefs present new creations and traditional specialities.

Further south along the Côte lies the city of Beaune, Burgundy's wine capital and the centre of wine shipping for the whole region. It is a small city, surrounded by ramparts, its buildings constructed from honey-coloured stone. The most famous of these is the Hôtel Dieu, its roof a spectacular confection of turrets and gables decorated with lozenges of multi-coloured tiles. Most streets in the old town are closed to cars making it possible for cafés, restaurants and shops to spill out on to the street. Wine is omnipresent: there are wine shops and cellars, a wine museum, a wine information bureau and antique and souvenir shops with wine as their main motif. Underneath the city is an amazing network of cellars, some of which date back to early medieval times.

The wine festival of *Les Trois Glorieuses* is held over three days in November. The first event is a candlelit dinner at Clos Vougeot, just outside Beaune, on Saturday. On Sunday the annual auction of the wines of the Hospices de Beaune takes place in the *halles* in front of the Hôtel Dieu. The bids are indicated by lighting candles: once no more candles are lit the lot has been sold. The Hospices own fifty-eight hectares of vines, mostly in Côte de Beaune. The festival ends with a literary lunch which takes place on Monday in Meursault.

ABOVE Much of central Beaune and Dijon has been closed to traffic, which has added to the pleasures of strolling in the streets or stopping for a drink in a café.
OPPOSITE, BELOW LEFT AND RIGHT Shopping on rue de la Liberté, one of Dijon's main shopping streets; a market stall.
BELOW LEFT Window-shopping for wine in Beaune.
BELOW Turrets and finials crown the multicoloured roof of the Hospices de Beaune.

The rich pasturelands of the plains and gently undulating hills provide grazing for herds of dairy and beef cattle. Cheeses such as those of Cîteaux, a form of which has been made since medieval times, and Epoisses, are justly famous. They are best complemented by a strong red Burgundy wine such as Pommard.

To the north of Dijon lies the Plateau de Langres, which borders the Champagne region. It is known for its cheese of the same name and as the birthplace of the *cocotte minute* – the pressure cooker – which was first made in an old ironmongery in Selongey in 1953.

To the east is the Châtillonais, where dark forests and hills harbour the source of the Seine. Abundant streams mean fertile lands. Not as populated now as they once were, the forests have the largest herds of deer in France and the streams are being repopulated with trout. In the part of southern Châtillonais, known as the Duesmois, one comes across places such as Aignay-le-Duc, Jours-les-Baigneux, Villaines-les-Duesmois and Frolois; once towns of some importance with imposing castles belonging to the dukes of Burgundy, they are now in decline, lost among winding country roads.

In these rural areas most farms are self-sufficient: cows provide milk for domestic consumption or for the making of cheeses; vegetables and fruit trees are grown in the potager; fowl, rabbits and pigs provide meat for the table. Many of the smaller villages have a market to which local producers bring their goods. In Aignay-le-Duc, the tiny market takes place on Fridays in front of the thirteenth-century church of Saint Peter and Saint Paul. Farmers' wives sell delicious fresh cheeses and cream, eggs, free-range chickens and produce from their gardens. At one stall a local producer, Madame Magerand, brings her fresh cows' milk cheeses, fromage frais and crème fraîche, as well as free-range guinea fowl, chickens, rabbits, terrines and pâtés. Nearby the local beekeeper sells honey and bunches of dried flowers.

Over the hills to the west, beyond Villaines-en-Duesmois, stands my favourite Cistercian abbey, Fontenay, set in a small valley through which a shallow river meanders. Charolais and Friesian cattle graze in the lush and peaceful meadows. The marshlands were drained and the abbey built by a handful of monks in 1130. Today Fontenay is a private residence but one can tour the grounds and visit the old bakery, the kitchen, the grain store, the large dovecote, the twelfth-century iron foundry and the draughty but elegant monks' dormitory.

ABOVE Vines in early summer near Corgoloin, between Beaune and Nuits-Saint-Georges. This village marks the end of the appellation Côte de Nuits.
OPPOSITE TOP Sylvain Mansuy breeds snails outdoors, where they cluster under pieces of wood for shelter.
OPPOSITE CENTRE Janine Verdier's snail shop is an institution in Dijon. She sells fresh and tinned snails and gives advice on their preparation.

RIGHT Possibly the finest of all remaining Cistercian abbeys, Fontenay is protected by UNESCO. The monastery church, seen at the centre of the picture, is remarkable for the dignified sobriety of its architecture.
FAR RIGHT A hamlet surrounded by the cereal fields of the Duesmois.

SNAILS

Most abbeys once had snail parks where small vine snails (*Helix pomatia*), a wild species which cannot be bred, were fed on aromatic plants and lettuces before being eaten. The gathering of snails from the vines in late spring was, until relatively recently, part of the rural cycle. This not only ensured that the vines were protected from the ravages of the snails but also provided a delicious windfall which was eagerly awaited. This tradition, along with the snails, has been killed off by the use of pesticides.

The snails served in most restaurants are *Helix aspersa*, a North African species. Larger than the local species, they are relatively easy to breed. One man who does so is Sylvain Mansuy, an ex-electrician and a newcomer to heliculture. He is one of only thirty people who raise snails in France. His snail park covers an area about the size of two tennis courts, enclosed by low walls and shrouded in fine plastic mesh to keep out predators. Within the walls, in neat rows, are hundreds of short lengths of wood, leaning against one another in inverted 'Vs'. Underneath are strips of grass and fine irrigation tubes. When Sylvain removed one of the lengths of wood, this curious construction began to make sense to me: nestling on the underside were hundreds of tiny snails. Raised indoors and transferred to the park once they have grown a soft shell, they are fed soya and protein. The snails remain in the park until they are ready to be eaten at six months old. They are then taken indoors and starved for up to one month, during which time they hibernate. They are starved because they will eat anything, some of which might be harmful to human beings.

Once they are ready for eating, the snails are cleaned and cooked in a vegetable stock with carrots, white wine, turnips, leeks, onions, thyme and bayleaf. Sylvain Mansuy preserves them in glass jars as he believes they can be tainted by the metallic taste of tins. During the winter he prepares the classic *escargots à la Bourgignonne*, snails in a garlic and parsley butter. The components of snail butters are closely-kept secrets, but Sylvain revealed that he makes his from a combination of butter, parsley, garlic, shallots, aniseed, salt, pepper, mustard and cream. He also prepares snails in puff pastry as hors d'oeuvres.

Madame Janine Verdier is the owner of the specialist snail shop in the Dijon market, next to Porcheret, the cheese shop. She was three years old when her mother bought the shop in 1937, and her family continue to sell both jam and snails to this day; all sizes of tinned snails are stocked and fresh snails prepared *à la Bourgignonne* are sold all year round except in the summer, when the warm weather makes it difficult to keep them fresh.

Tinned snails should be pre-cooked in a vegetable and white wine stock before butter is added. Snails prepared *à la Bourguignonne* are best baked quickly in a very hot oven until the butter foams; overcooking them turns them to rubber. Madame Kuzma, who runs a *ferme auberge* in Frolois, is often called upon to make 'snail feasts' consisting of six courses of different snail dishes for snail lovers. Madame Kuzma (see page 83) serves them in puff pastry while restaurateur Jean-Pierre Silva in Bouilland (see page 80) serves them on a bed of cooked nettles, a recipe which Henri Vincenot, a well-known local author, recalls from his youth in his novel, *The Snail Pope*. In this book, the Snail Pope is the nickname of the 'village idiot' who raises a gigantic snail.

MOUTARDE DE DIJON

AU VINAIGRE FIN

DE BOURGOGNE

QUELLE!!! BONNE MOUTARDE

Garantie

Pure

ÉTABLISSEMENTS

FALLOT & C.ie

Usine Electrique Moderne

BEAUNE

PRÈS

DIJON

IMP. DELCEY-DOLE

MUSTARD

On the outskirts of Beaune stands a small factory which was opened in 1840 by the Fallot family to press oil and manufacture mustard. It continues to make traditional-style mustard and sells aromatic vinegars, gherkins and pickled onions. Marc Desarmeniens, the handsome grandson of the original Monsieur Fallot, has taken over the day-to-day running of the business from his father, but the latter, from an adjacent desk, still keeps a watchful eye on proceedings. On the walls of their office are framed collections of old mustard labels, and mustard pots line the window ledge.

The old equipment of the Fallot factory has been retained in parts of the building. The beautiful large sieves and millstones of the last century are to be reconditioned and, in time, will form a mustard museum. In central Dijon, at the Maille shop, one can see a fascinating and extensive display of antique mustard pots made of porcelain, wood, glass, metal or Italian earthenware.

It is believed that the Romans introduced the mustard seed to Burgundy, but it was only in the thirteenth century that mention was first made of it being used. The dukes of Burgundy travelled with their own mustard barrels and are known to have sent them as gifts. Mustard seed is still grown in Burgundy but not in large quantities and the Fallot factory imports the grains from Canada.

The French word for mustard is used in a variety of expressions of which the most famous is '*la moutarde me monte au nez*' (literally translated as 'mustard is coming up my nose', it means 'I am seeing red'). One has just this feeling when eating a strong dose of mustard: it tickles the nose and tears come to the eyes, which is precisely what happened when I went into the small Fallot factory. Tears were soon running down my cheeks due to the acrid atmosphere created by the release of the mustard oils.

Mustard used to be made by pounding the seeds in a mortar, but nowadays the seeds are crushed by machines operating at high speed. The friction creates a high temperature and this releases essential oils, most of which are lost in the process. At the Fallot factory this loss is limited because the grinding is done at slow speed between flint stones incised with opposite grooves. Mustard is made with the seeds of the black mustard plant (*Brassica nigra*) and the yellow mustard plant (*B. juncea*), together with water, vinegar, salt, spices such as turmeric, and anti-oxidizers. Vinegar is now used in place of verjuice (the acidic juice of green grapes) since verjuice is no longer produced in large enough quantities.

In traditional mustard the seeds are not sieved after being ground and the paste has a coarse texture. Dijon mustard is made by the slow crushing of the mustard seeds. The seeds are removed so that the resulting mustard is fine in texture and a rich yellow in colour. It is sold with or without the addition of green peppercorns, white wine, tarragon or blackcurrant. Mustard is not protected by AOC regulations and consequently Dijon mustard can come from anywhere, so it is worth checking the small print on the label.

Mustard loses its flavour rather quickly when subjected to high temperatures, so it is best to add it at the end of the cooking process or top up the quantity used in such dishes as *Lapin à la Dijonnaise* (see recipe on page 88).

ANIS DE FLAVIGNY

The beneficial effects of aniseed were known to the Romans (Julius Caesar used it to treat dysentery when the Romans laid siege to Alesia) and aniseed is a main spice of pain d'épices. The factory of Anis de Flavigny, which occupies part of the abbey of Flavigny, has been owned by the Troubat family since 1923. Legend has it that the recipe for the factory's aniseed balls was invented by nuns who settled at Flavigny in 1600. However the tall, kindly Monsieur Troubat believes that the recipe was invented by an earlier community of monks. The aniseed balls are coated with several layers of sugar syrup. This process takes one month and fifty hours of machine time; if done by hand it would take six months.

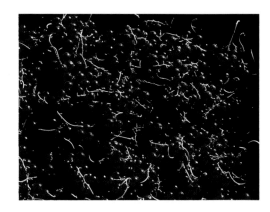

LEFT AND RIGHT The best blackcurrants and red-currants of Burgundy grow in the Hautes Côtes. *BELOW* The peaceful village of Concoeur-et-Corboin in the Hautes Côtes de Nuits offers a welcome retreat from the noisy, crowded stretch of the route des Vins between Beaune and Dijon. Famed for their fruit, the small villages of this area are turning once more to grape-growing. Their history can be traced in a museum in the town of Reulle-Vergy, where a blackcurrant fête is held at the beginning of July.

BLACKCURRANTS

One of the most emblematic of Burgundian drinks is kir, a mixture of white wine (usually Aligoté) and *crème de cassis*. Blackcurrants were brought to Burgundy by the monks of Cîteaux who grew them for the medicinal qualities of their leaves. The fruit is now known to be high in vitamin C and is drunk as a hot toddy during the winter months in the Hautes-Côtes. In the latter part of the nineteenth century *viticulteurs*, their vines destroyed by phylloxera, turned to blackcurrants to revive their economic fortunes. The fruit was grown for the purpose of transforming it into *crème, liqueur* or *sirop de cassis*. The finest fruit is grown on the Hautes-Côtes, where the soil is chalky and dry. The variety most commonly grown is the Gros Noir de Bourgogne, which is sweet and aromatic.

In recent years the market has been flooded with cheap and poor quality Eastern European blackcurrants. In some instances blackcurrant farmers have become producers of *crème de cassis* (see right). One such family is the Oliviers.

The family of Christian and Chantale Olivier have lived in Concoeur-et-Corboin, a small village in the Haute-Côtes above Nuits-Saint-Georges, for over five generations. They had always grown grapes and only turned to growing blackcurrants when phylloxera destroyed the vineyards. Now the Oliviers grow blackcurrants, raspberries and strawberries and produce their own *crèmes de cassis, framboise* and *fraise*. Recently they have begun to re-plant the vines.

Madame Olivier is part of a group called 'Ecrivains Paysans' consisting of one hundred and twenty writers throughout rural France. She has had some of her own poetry and short stories published and is ferocious about defending the 'peasant' way of life. She hankers after the ancient way of living and the self-sufficiency that farms in the past used to enjoy. She is also a good source for old regional recipes which she cooks for her guests at their *ferme auberge*. In her poetic way, Madame Olivier explained to me how the blackcurrant plants and the vines have become part of the collective unconscious of the farmers in the Hautes-Côtes.

CHARCUTERIE

Daniel Borgeot, a butcher, *charcutier, traiteur* and member of the Confrérie de Saint-Antoine, has been working in the meat trade since the age of fourteen and has had his own shop in Santenay for twenty-six years. His brother, also a *charcutier*, has a shop in Seurre, and they exchange tips and recipes over the telephone.

Daniel Borgeot's specialities are *jambon persillé à l'ancienne, jambon persillé* (see recipe on page 89), for which he won a gold medal in 1993 and his own dry-cured ham, which is marinated in Santenay wine lees, or sediment. He also sells *andouilles* (cooked and ready to eat) and *andouillettes* (which need steaming and recooking). When I visited him, he showed me the buckets where the strips of pigs' intestines were soaking before being prepared into *andouilles*.

CRÈME DE CASSIS

Crème and liqueur de cassis are both made by macerating blackcurrants in alcohol. The crème contains four hundred grams of sugar per litre and the liqueur one hundred grams. Home producers usually add more sugar per litre and use better quality fruits than those used in factory production. The best cassis has the highest degree of alcohol and the most fruit and sugar. It is known as Crème de Cassis de Dijon only if made in Dijon, but the fruits can come from anywhere. Made on an industrial basis since the mid-eighteenth century by Dijon distillers Lejay Lagoutte, cassis was traditionally drunk by women, while the men drank marc or fine. In the tiny village of Arcenant, Jean-Baptiste Joannet and his son Giles prepare raspberry, blackcurrant, redcurrant, blackberry and strawberry liqueurs. Giles has taken to making an old favourite, liqueur de prunelle, *with the stones of small, wild, yellow plums. The fruits are macerated in large vats of alcohol for four to six weeks before being bottled. Giles does everything by hand: he even seals the bottles by hand, dipping them in wax.*

BELOW *A 'modern' jambon persillé*
displayed in Daniel Borgeot's shop in Santenay.
A winner of the annual gold medal
for this dish, he also produces a
'traditional' variant in
which the pieces are finely chopped
and the dish is presented in small glass bowls.
BOTTOM *Saucissons hanging to dry*
in the cellar under Borgeot's charcuterie.
BOTTOM RIGHT *Air-cured ham (right) can*
also be bought soaked in the lees
of Santenay wine (left).

To prepare hams, Borgeot buys whole pigs, selecting the best hindquarters. The meat rests for forty-eight hours, and is then rubbed every day for a week with salt, herbs and spices, among them thyme, bayleaf, mustard, juniper berries, and saltpetre. Stored in a cool room, the meat is brushed with cold water for one month and dried for six to eight months in a *séchoir* (drying room). Borgeot prepares about two hundred and fifty hams per year and customers often buy whole hams from him on their way back from holidays in the south. He has at least one hundred and fifty in store at any given time, labelled according to the day they were made – hence the numbers that are stamped on them – and recorded in a little black book.

Borgeot found an old recipe for dry ham marinated in Santenay wine lees and now prepares a few hams in this way. Marinated for a month, the meat is then dried and the bone taken out after eight months; the ham is then pressed in a large metal mould to regain its shape. It can be kept refrigerated whole for up to a year. He advises that, once the ham is cut, it is best not to remove the fat as it helps to preserve the meat.

In his spotless kitchen above the shop Borgeot is developing new products: prepared food such as *galets du mont de Sène* (hand-rolled salami with nuts, raisins or pepper) and traditional dry *saucissons*, *judru* and *rosette*, which have to dry for a month.

He calls his *séchoir* his second wife as he spends so much time there, checking that the *saucissons* and the hams are drying correctly, that the temperature (which should be at around thirteen to fourteen degrees Centigrade) is constant and humidity is kept at the correct level.

A lively, friendly but no-nonsense man, Daniel Borgeot takes pride in his trade and is very successful, but he explains that in the rest of Burgundy *charcutiers* are closing down, put out of business by industrialized food production. They cannot compete with modern methods and the scale of factory production, but they are also prevented by law from selling their meat in other parts of France, or to restaurants. Were they able to do so perhaps more of these traditional *charcutiers* would flourish.

OPPOSITE LEFT *An array of Burgundy cheeses at*
the well-known cheese shop of
Porcheret in Dijon, most of which are matured
in Porcheret's own cellars.
In the centre is a Citeaux cheese, surrounded by
tiny fresh and dried goats' cheeses
(Boutons de Culottes) and, clockwise from top
centre, a tall, cylindrical Charollais; a
Soumaintrain; a Langres cheese; two goat's
cheeses; an Aisy Cendré; three
Mâconnais and, top left, an Epoisses.
OPPOSITE CENTRE *Porcheret makes and sells a*
fresh cheese topped with savory
and pink peppercorns.

CHEESES OF THE COTE D'OR

There are almost as many cheeses in Burgundy as there are villages and farms, and many of them do not even have names. Some carry the name of their village and have become famous all over France. Cheeses from other regions of France, such as Chaource, Brie, Comté and *crottins* made from goats' cheese, are also made in Burgundy, but have no claim to being Burgundian. The region's most important cheeses are Epoisses, described by Brillat-Savarin, the nineteenth-century lawyer, philosopher and gastronome, as 'the king of cheeses', and Citeaux, made by Cistercian monks at the abbey of the same name. Epoisses is a soft cows' milk cheese which is washed in marc. It is the only Burgundian cheese to have been awarded an *appellation d'origine contrôlée* (AOC). Citeaux, which has an orange rind, resembles a very creamy and mild Reblochon. It can be bought only at the abbey shop or at specialist cheese shops such as Porcheret in Dijon, as production is small.

Like charcuteries, few cheese shops have managed to survive as they are being squeezed out by the giant supermarkets. One which has is that of Simone Porcheret in Dijon. Opened in 1964 by one of the few women to obtain the grade of Maître Fromager in the Cheese Confrérie of Saint-Uguzon, the shop now belongs to the Gaugry family. The family are cheese-makers of equal repute in Gevrey-Chambertin, where they run La Laiterie de La Côte and make Ami du Chambertin. François Gaugry, the son of the family, abandoned a promising career in engineering in Argentina to take over the running of Porcheret. The shop has traditionally given pride of place to farmhouse cheeses, which are aged in their own cellars. Some cheeses, such as Meule de Beaufort, need six to eight months to mature. Porcheret stocks a total of two hundred and fifty varieties of goats' cheese during the year and all thirty-two of the current AOC cheeses.

Gaugry believes in encouraging people to rediscover the subtleties of flavour which are being lost in the move towards mass production. In sessions organized by the Conseil National des Arts Culinaires, he gives lessons on flavour to children in schools and even teaches them how to make a white cheese. His shop sells cheese platters with a wide variety of cheeses which can make up an entire meal.

FARMHOUSE EPOISSES AT LA FERME DU COLOMBIER

Epoisses, one of the finest examples of Burgundy cheeses, is made in the Auxois region according to a method devised by Cistercian monks and handed down from mother to daughter for many generations. Nearby at Pris-les-Arnay, dairy farmer Hervé Pinczon du Sel keeps fifty Montbéliarde cows which provide milk for the Epoisses (above) made by his wife Odile. The small, cylindrical cheeses are first moulded and then drained, salted and dried. In the early stages of ripening they are washed twice a week with water; then with a mixture of water and marc and eventually, in the last stages, with undiluted marc. The whole process is delicate and time-consuming, but Madame Pinczon du Sel says she feels at peace with the world as she works in her dairy listening to Mozart. Epoisses de Bourgogne is not comparable with the factory-made cheese called Epoisses, a fresh cheese similar to a bland cream cheese with a rocou cover produced by an orange colourant. The name Epoisses is currently the subject of litigation.

ABOVE The nineteenth-century castle at Aloxe-Corton. The red and white wines of Corton were favoured by such illustrious figures as Voltaire, Maupassant and John F. Kennedy.
OPPOSITE ABOVE Grape-picking at the Clos des Perrières near Pommard.
OPPOSITE BELOW LEFT The first green buds of Pinot Noir grapes.
OPPOSITE BELOW CENTRE Grapes missed by the harvesters. In the past these would have been gleaned by villagers to make their own wine.
OPPOSITE BELOW RIGHT Gamay grapes.

LA ROUTE DES VINS

As you take La Route des Vins from Dijon and work your way southwards to Beaune, the land and small villages become increasingly charged with the atmosphere and culture of wine-making. Neat rows of vines line the road, tended to perfection like Japanese gardens. In the distance, as the vine-covered slopes of the Côte start to rise, to the right of the road are landmarks such as Clos Vougeot, one of the first properties owned by the abbey of Cîteaux, with cellars and wine presses dating back to the twelfth century, and the castle of Aloxe-Corton, with its bright yellow, black and red zigzag-tiled roof.

At the entrance to most villages stands a monument – an old wooden *pressoir* on a plinth, a strangely moving testimony to the importance of grapes. Men and women can be seen working slowly and methodically in the June heat, up and down the rows of vines. The manual work entailed in working in the vineyards is sometimes assisted by tall tractors, with the cabin built high enough to reach over the rows of vines. Many small domaines, however, continue to tend the vines by hand because tractors, although they do not represent a huge investment, can damage the vines. Most *vignerons* or wine-growers will know their plants well and anticipate any reaction to changing conditions.

Classification of the vineyards was established in the eighteenth century with a list of the best wine-producing villages and *clos*. A study made in the 1860s became the basis of the law of 1935 which established the AOC (see page 25), deemed necessary to protect the consumer from fraud.

What makes the wine of Burgundy particular? The answer is a combination of three factors: the *cépage* (grape type), the *terroir* (land) and the *climat* (macro- and micro-climatic conditions). The chosen *cépage* is grafted on to an American root variety which is resistant to phylloxera and which gives it strength. The four principal *cépages* in Burgundy are the Pinot, Gamay, Chardonnay and Aligoté. The Pinot gives Burgundy its reputation for great red wines. Its juice has no colour; all the colour lies in the skins which, during fermentation, impart a powerful red hue to the wine. The black Gamay, with white juice, produces the fine red wines of the Beaujolais and the Mâconnais. From the Chardonnay grape come the great white wines of the Côte d'Or, the Mâconnais and Chablis. The Aligoté, an ancient Burgundian *cépage*, produces refreshing, if acidic, white wines such as those of Bouzeron, which are best drunk young or in a kir.

Grapes prefer rocky soil which drains easily and warms quickly. In the Côte d'Or the land is a mixture of chalky clay and limestone, but there are local variations which determine the characteristics and quality of the wines and distinguish *clos* from *clos*. Each year about twenty thousand different wines are produced in Burgundy. On the upper slopes of the Côte are the *grands crus* and the *premiers crus*; around the villages' slightly sloping terrain are the *appellations communales* and, towards the plain, the *appellations régionales*.

Grapes need light and warmth. In Burgundy's extremes of heat and cold the orientation of the Côtes is crucial in protecting the vines from frost, and winds, allowing them to soak up the sun and in preventing the stocks from becoming waterlogged.

Lastly, it is the way in which all these factors are exploited by the *vignerons*, both in

tending the grapes and in making the wine, which gives each vintage its distinctivness. Before a wine can go on sale it must undergo both tasting and chemical analysis at the INAO laboratory (see page 25). This is a period of anxiety for all wine-makers, for the tasting will determine whether or not the wine is to retain its *appellation*.

Despite its reputation for great red wines Burgundy now produces and sells slightly more white than red, leaving aside Beaujolais, which is in a category of its own. More people live a sedentary life nowadays than in the past, and there is a corresponding tendency towards lighter food and wine. An abundance of produce all year round also means an increase in the demand for a range of accompanying wines throughout the year. Most French wines are subject, like everything else, to cycles of fashion, but those of Burgundy are different: they are great wines which need to be kept for a long time and producers cannot respond rapidly to an increase in demand. Chablis has the good fortune that it is always popular.

CONFRERIES

Wine confréries, *or brotherhoods, are modelled on the Sociétés de Secours Mutuel of the nineteenth century, established to offer protection to wine-growers: if a* vigneron *was sick he could count on the help of his fellow* vignerons *to tend to his vines.*

This spirit of solidarity has filtered down to the present day and many vignerons *help each other at harvest time as well as meeting to discuss methodology.*

One such organization, the Confrérie des Chevaliers du Tastevin, was created in 1934 in an effort to combat the slump in the wine trade by increasing exports.

Its members meet in the castle of Clos Vougeot, built by the monks of Cîteaux in the twelfth century and used by its abbots until 1791.

In a special ceremony new members, wearing robes of scarlet and gold, vow to defend and promote the wines and gastronomy of Burgundy.

Many other confréries *now exist, each one with its own calendar of annual celebrations. The most important are the Feast of Saint Vincent Tournante in January, the feast to mark the beginning of the grape harvest in September, and Les Trois Glorieuses (page 65).*

JEAN-MARC ROULOT

*Jean-Marc Roulot is the fourth in line of a dynasty of wine-makers and distillers in Meursault,
the centre of the white-wine-growing district of the Côte d'Or. He produces a range
of excellent white wines from Aligoté and Chardonnay grapes, including the* appellation *Meursault
Les Tessons Clos de Mon Plaisir and the* premier crus *Meursault Perrières and Charmes.
His vineyard, covering more than eleven hectares in five villages, yields a relatively
large production for Burgundy and his wines are much in demand.
Meursault produces more white wines than most villages in Burgundy, and the quality of its
production is thought to be the highest. The grapes are carefully hand-picked in late September by
seasoned pickers. The work is hard and care is taken not to pick grapes which are underripe
or over-mature, in order to keep the taste of the wine pure. Pictured above and right are harvesting
scenes from the slopes of Meix Chavaux. Meals are convivial times for the group and are
often prepared by Madame Roulot and her daughter. They take care in choosing the best ingredients
and cook wholesome dishes to reward the pickers for their strenuous work.*

THE ROLE OF THE NEGOCIANT

Negociants (wine-merchants) have played a complex and historically important role in wine-making in Burgundy. In the past the *negociant* would purchase the raw material and transform, blend, bottle and, finally, ship the wine all over the world. Often a *negociant* would purchase the production of a single village, blending it and labelling it with the name of that village. Inevitably this meant that local variation was lost and most *vignerons* were simply growers of a crop. However, by the 1970s the situation began to change and greater numbers of *vignerons* began to make, bottle, store and sell directly to the consumer. *Vignerons* now sell up to fifty per cent of the wine made in Burgundy by direct sale, thereby increasing the range of wines available to the consumer. *Negociants,* such as Bouchard and Drouhin in Beaune, have diversified their interests and, in the last thirty years, have increased their holdings of vineyards from which they produce some extremely fine wines.

COTE DE NUITS

The Côte de Nuits region stretches southwards from Fixin, just below Dijon, to Corgoloin, above Beaune. In 1680 King Louis XIV became ill and doctors ordered him to drink the wines of the Côte de Nuits to regain his strength; the wines have been famous ever since.

In '*Les Mémoires d'un Touriste',* Stendhal writes of a journey through the Côte d'Or and of tasting wines of the Clos Vougeot. He describes a discussion that took place about the merits of harvesting the grapes in a specific direction and observes that, after two hours of tasting, he began to be able to distinguish the characteristics that identified each wine.

Every few years a wine of exceptional quality is produced in the Côte de Nuits. In the weeks before the harvest the *vignerons* discuss the likelihood of rain, wind and even hot sun at the wrong moment, all of which might damage the crop. So it is with an infectious sense of trepidation and excitement that the first tasting of each wine takes place.

DOMAINE PRIEURE-ROCH

On the main road through Nuits-Saint-Georges, which is flanked by elegant mansions, a break in the grey stone walls reveals the large glass doors of the offices of the Domaine Prieuré-Roch. I came here to see Henri-Frédéric Roch and to learn more about organic wines and the renowned estate of Romanée-Conti. A producer of remarkable wines, Romanée-Conti is known to have been harvested from the Le Clos des Cloux in 1512. Bought by the Prince de Conti in 1760, the estate covered precisely the same area then as it does now.

Born with a *tastevin* (a cup used for wine-tasting) in his mouth, Roch admits that he has been lucky. His grandfather is Henri Leroy, from the family of shippers of Auxey-Duresses, who are part-owners of the Domaine Romanée-Conti. He became co-director of this domaine recently but was already making his own wine in small vineyards such as Clos de

MARC AND FINE DE BOURGOGNE

Once the grapes have been pressed to make wine, the residue is collected and kept aside until winter. This is then placed in sealed vats to ferment before being distilled. The distilled liquid is aged in new oak casks for ten to twelve years.

The result of this process is a spirit called marc. In order to be awarded an official seal of approval (appellation reglementée) the alcoholic content of the distilled marc must be no lower than forty degrees and no higher than seventy-one degrees.

Fine is sometimes distilled from wine but in Burgundy it is made with the lees, or sediment, of the wine left in the cask.

New laws and taxes, as well as the time needed for distillation, have meant that these spirits are chiefly made by large distilleries. The family of Jean-Marc Roulot were distillers before they became wine-makers (see opposite). Jean-Marc remembers when his father and grandfather, who were travelling distillers, spent the winter months journeying from village to village with their old still to make fine.

ABOVE This striking label, so different from traditional labels, has been specifically designed to catch the eye of the supermarket shopper.

ABOVE AND TOP The Clos-Vougeot vineyards cover fifty hectares and have over seventy owners.
ABOVE RIGHT Sisters Chantal and Marie-Andrée Gerbet are among a handful of women who produce excellent wines.
LEFT AND RIGHT Wine-makers in Burgundy still use very traditional methods and ageing wines in oak barrels remains an essential part of the process. Barrels made at the Tonnellerie Damy in Meursault are exported worldwide.
OPPOSITE Jean-Claude Rateau (top) continues the family tradition of wine-making, and now produces wine by the Steiner method. The wine press dating from the early twentieth century (bottom) has largely been superseded by computer-activated presses.

Vougeot. Few young men have had the opportunity to acquire as much knowledge of wine as he has from his family and the masters of Romanée-Conti. An articulate man, once Roch starts talking about wine he will not stop, although he says wines should speak for themselves.

At the domaine grass grows among the vines, the branches are thinned out in order to concentrate the grapes, yeasts are natural and a filter is rarely used. Roch remembers taking an aggressive American wine-buyer to his vineyard before a wine-tasting. The buyer was so impressed by the state of the vineyard that he placed an order on the strength of it, saying that a man who tended his vines in this way would be sure to have excellent wines.

DOMAINE JEAN-CLAUDE RATEAU

Jean-Claude Rateau speaks of his biodynamic wine quietly but with passion. Seated at a wooden table in the Chemin des Mariages outside Beaune, in a grassy clearing among the vines, he explains the conditions required by the plants in order to grow well.

Based on techniques pioneered by Rudolf Steiner in the 1920s, this complicated concept, one step beyond organic agriculture, operates according to a special calendar. As in organic agriculture, no chemical weedkillers or pesticides are used. A healthy soil structure is built up by using organic compost and applying minute quantities of powdered minerals. The year-long tasks of the *vigneron*, as well as all the processes of winemaking, are done by hand following a specific timetable linked with the phases of the moon and the stars. This allows the soil to regain its natural structure and to be free from chemicals.

Rateau started out with one hectare in 1979, and now has a total of eight. His Beaune wines have a taste reminiscent of *grillottes* (sour cherries). *Premier cru* Les Reversées 1990 is delicious, as is his wine from 1902 vines (which make only fifteen hectolitres per hectare).

MARIE-ANDREE AND CHANTAL GERBET

In 1983 sisters Marie-Andrée and Chantal Gerbet took over the wine-growing estate established in 1947 by their father François. François Gerbet remembers that when he bought the Clos aux Réas, then a potato field in Vosne-Romanée, everyone told him it was too chalky for grapes to be grown. He has since proved them wrong. His daughters, in adopting the latest vine-tending techniques, hope to improve upon their father's traditional methods.

Tall, blonde Marie-Andrée was bitten early by the wine-making bug. Having studied oenology, she joined her parents in the business in 1972. She remembers helping in the vineyards at eight years old and spending school holidays working on the estate. Following the general movement in Burgundy, the sisters have started bottling their own wine and selling direct to the consumer, and have made a number of innovations in wine-making. The vineyards cover thirteen hectares with a large proportion of production consisting of very good Bourgogne Hautes Côtes de Nuits, with some Vosne-Romanée *premier cru* 'Les Petits Monts', *grand cru* Echezeaux and Clos Vougeot making up most of the balance.

LE VIEUX MOULIN

BOUILLAND 21420, TEL 80 21 51 16

Vines continue along the Hautes Côtes a few kilometres from Nuits-Saint-Georges, but behind the ridge is another world. The roads climb through densely wooded valleys to high, tranquil meadows which surround the spectacular ruins of the abbey of Sainte Marguerite, founded by Augustine monks in the ninth century. Standing amidst the few houses of Bouilland is the restaurant run by Jean-Pierre Silva and his wife Isabelle (illustrated left). Although they come from southern France, their menu is largely Burgundian in inspiration. Self-taught, Jean-Pierre is a perfectionist who loves cooking and dreams of creating unique meals every night for friends. His dishes are complex and exciting, his Raviolis Bourguignons (filled with Coq au Vin*) delicious and his spit-roasted meats – capon, guinea fowl, beef and lamb – a treat.*

GATEAU D'ECREVISSES ET FROMAGE DE CHEVRE BLANC, COULIS AUX POIVRONS ROUGES

Fresh Goats' Cheese with Crayfish, Served with a Red Pepper Sauce

This is an elegant starter to prepare for a warm day. You can buy the crayfish already cooked if you are in a hurry. (Illustrated left)

SERVES 4

48 crayfish or large prawns, bought fresh or cooked in a court bouillon
fish or vegetable stock, to cover (optional)
2tbsp single cream
small bunch of fresh chives, finely chopped
4tbsp olive oil
salt and freshly ground black pepper
200g/7oz fresh goats' cheese
young spinach leaves or purslane

FOR THE COULIS
1 red pepper
3tbsp olive oil

If the crayfish are fresh, prepare them by peeling them and removing the intestinal vein along the tail. Add them to a large pan of boiling stock and cook for 5-7 minutes. Drain and refresh under cold water. Set aside.

Preheat the oven to 190°C/375°F/gas mark 5.

To prepare the coulis, roast the red pepper whole by placing it directly on the oven shelf for 45 minutes or until both sides are charred and the flesh collapses easily when gently squeezed. When ready, place it in a paper bag, seal the bag and leave to cool.

Once the pepper has cooled, peel off the skin with a small knife and take out the seeds and the stem. Coarsely chop the flesh and purée with the 3 tablespoons of olive oil in a food processor or blender, adding a little water if the mixture is too thick.

In a bowl whisk together the cream, chives, 4 tablespoons of oil and seasoning. Crumble the goats' cheese and mix into the cream.

Mould the mixture into 4 even rounds and place on a baking tray. Chill for 30 minutes until firm.

Arrange the crayfish around the cheese, garnish with spinach or purslane, and dribble the red pepper sauce round the plates.

SANDRE MARINE A LA BOURGUIGNONNE

Zander Marinated in White Wine and Marc
(Illustrated right, above)

SERVES 4

4 x 175g/6½ oz fillets of zander, with
the skins left on
4 leeks whites
45g/1½ oz butter
4tbsp single cream, to garnish
salt and freshly ground black pepper

FOR THE MARINADE

250ml/8fl oz white Burgundy wine
4tbsp marc or brandy
1 carrot, finely sliced
1 onion, very finely chopped
1tbsp butter
½ bay leaf
1 sprig fresh thyme
2tbsp olive oil
small bunch of parsley, finely chopped
small bunch of fresh chives, finely chopped

The day before cooking mix all the marinade ingredients together in a large, non-metallic bowl, cover and leave overnight in a cool place for the flavours to infuse.

Simmer the leek whites in salt water until tender, then refresh under cold, running water. Cut the leeks once lengthways, separate the leaves, cut into thin strips and reserve.

Preheat the oven to 160°C/325°F/gas mark 3.

Put the fillets into the marinade for 10 minutes. Remove with a slotted spoon, then season. Reserve the marinade. Melt 15g/½ oz of butter in a frying pan with an oven-proof handle and cook the fillets, skin sides down, over a low heat for 8 minutes. Cover and transfer the pan to the oven for 10 minutes. Arrange the leeks on 4 oven-proof plates, cover with the fish and return to the oven.

Mix the 2 tablespoons of reserved marinade, 4 tablespoons of water and the remaining butter in a saucepan. Bring to the boil and simmer for 1-2 minutes to thicken. Season to taste. Spoon the sauce over each fillet and top with 1 tablespoon of cream just before serving.

COMPOTE DE TOMATES AUX FRUITS ROUGES

Tomato Compôte Served with Red Fruits

This unusual way of serving tomatoes makes an attractive dessert. (Illustrated right, below)

SERVES 4

450g/1lb tomatoes, peeled, seeded and diced
250g/8½ oz sugar
2 cinnamon sticks
100g/3½ oz puff pastry, thawed if frozen
½ tbsp icing sugar
2 large punnets of raspberries, strawberries
or redcurrants, or a mixture
few drops balsamic vinegar (optional)

To make the compôte simmer the tomatoes, sugar and cinnamon in a saucepan, stirring until the liquid has evaporated. Leave to cool.

Preheat the oven to 200°C/400°F/gas mark 6.

Roll out the pastry as thinly as possible on a lightly floured surface and cut into 4 triangles measuring 4cm/1¾in on the base and 10cm/4in along the sides. Place on a baking sheet and prick with a fork. Bake for 5 minutes until puffed up and golden. Meanwhile preheat the grill to high.

Sift the icing sugar over the puff pastry triangles and put under the grill to glaze and brown for a few minutes.

To serve, spoon the compôte into the centre of 4 plates and scatter the soft fruit around the edge. Sprinkle a few drops of vinegar around the fruit and then place a pastry triangle over the compôte. Serve immediately.

SOUPE AU VIN

Red Wine Soup

Burgundian cooks have always appreciated how quick and easy soups are to make. In the past, a pot could be left simmering while the cook was busy tending to the animals or doing other farm chores. Some soups were as simple as pouring hot cream, water or wine over bread. A popular saying has it that,

La soupe à la Guillemette

Elle bout quand elle est faite.

In other words, Madame Guillemette's soup was ready as soon as the water boiled. It was eaten garnished with croutons and double cream which had been left to sit for eight days.

The last drops of a glass of wine are often added to any soup to give extra warmth on cold nights.

SERVES 4

2 carrots, finely diced
1 turnip, finely diced
1 leek white, thinly sliced
1 large onion, thinly sliced
1 ½ tbsp butter
400ml/14fl oz red Burgundy wine
1l/1 ¾ pt chicken stock
2tbsp tapioca (optional)
salt and freshly ground black pepper

Sauté the carrots, turnip, leek white and onion in the butter in a large saucepan for about 10 minutes. Add the wine, cover and simmer for 20 minutes. Add the stock, cover and simmer for a further 10 minutes. Season to taste.

If you wish to thicken the soup, sprinkle in the tapioca, mix well and simmer, uncovered, for 10 minutes.

Serve with a country-style bread, such as *pain du bûcheron* (see page 61).

OEUFS EN MEURETTE

Poached Eggs in Red Wine Sauce

The red wine sauce in this recipe can be adapted for a variety of meat or fish dishes. Prepare the sauce the day before and re-heat it while you are poaching the eggs.

SERVES 4

8 small, thin slices of *pain de campagne*
or baguette
2 garlic cloves, halved
55g/2oz butter
3tbsp white wine vinegar
8 eggs
small bunch of fresh chives, finely chopped

FOR THE SAUCE

100g/3 ½ oz streaky bacon or lardons
4 shallots, very finely chopped
55g/2oz butter
1 ½ tbsp plain flour
750ml/27fl oz red Burgundy wine
1 bouquet garni
salt and freshly ground black pepper

To make the sauce, put the bacon in a saucepan, cover with water and bring to the boil. Remove the bacon immediately, pat dry with paper towels and dice finely.

In a large saucepan, sauté the bacon and the shallots in the butter over a medium heat. When the shallots are translucent, stir in the flour and cook for about 5 minutes, stirring occasionally.

Take the saucepan off the heat and pour in the red wine, whisking well. Return to the heat, add the bouquet garni and simmer, uncovered, for 25 minutes. Season with salt and freshly ground black pepper to taste.

Preheat the oven to 120°C/250°F/gas mark ½.

Put 4 soup plates to warm. Rub the bread with the garlic cloves, then fry it in the butter until golden on both sides. Place 2 slices of bread in each of the soup plates.

Fill a large, shallow pan with water, almost to the top. Add the vinegar. Bring to the boil, then lower the heat and simmer. Crack the eggs gently into the pan, one by one. Try to keep track of the eggs you have put in first so you can take them out in the same order. Poach each egg for 3-4 minutes.

Using a slotted spoon, carefully transfer the eggs to a plate covered with paper towels to drain and trim the straggly ends off the whites.

Place an egg on each slice of bread and pour the sauce around the eggs. Sprinkle the eggs with chives and serve immediately.

ESCARGOTS EN CHAUSSURE LUTEE

Snails in Puff Pastry with a Hazelnut and Mushroom Sauce

Maryse Kuzma of the ferme auberge 'Les Comes' in Frolois makes six different snail dishes. This is a rich starter. (Illustrated right)

SERVES 4
4 shallots, finely chopped
1 garlic clove, crushed
1tbsp butter
200g/7oz mushrooms, thinly sliced
100ml/3 ½ fl oz white Burgundy wine
225ml/8fl oz single cream
250ml/8fl oz vegetable stock
55g/2oz hazelnuts, skinned and finely chopped
3 tomatoes, skinned and diced
1tbsp each of fresh chives, parsley and chervil, finely chopped
250g/8oz puff pastry, thawed if frozen
24 tinned snails, drained
1 egg yolk, lightly beaten
salt and freshly ground black pepper

Preheat the oven to 200°C/400°F/gas mark 6.

To make the sauce fry the shallots and the garlic in the butter, add the mushrooms and wine and cook for 5 minutes. Stir in the cream and stock, then boil for 3-4 minutes to reduce. Stir in the nuts, tomatoes and herbs and season.

Roll out the pastry on a lightly floured surface. Cut out 4 rounds big enough to overlap the tops of four 115g/4oz ramekins.

Spoon 6 snails into each ramekin, cover with sauce and the puff pastry. Seal the edges and glaze each top with the beaten egg yolk. Bake for 10 minutes or until the puff pastry has risen and is golden. Serve immediately.

CHAMPIGNONS A LA DIJONNAISE

Mushrooms in a Cream and Mustard Sauce

This dish is delicious as a sauce for pasta, with baked potatoes or to accompany fish, which can be transformed into Brochet à la Dijonnaise *by the addition of bacon. I was served mushrooms as a separate course by Madame Mouillefarine, in her lively country restaurant in Beaunotte. If wild mushrooms are in season, use a mixture. (Illustrated left)*

SERVES 4
450g/1lb mixed small button mushrooms, chanterelles and girolles, trimmed
juice of 1 lemon
2tbsp butter
2 shallots, finely chopped
3 sprigs of fresh thyme
100ml/3 ½ fl oz Burgundy white wine
250ml/8fl oz single cream
1 egg yolk
2tbsp Dijon mustard
salt and freshly ground black pepper
2tbsp finely chopped fresh parsley

Sprinkle the mushrooms with lemon juice and sauté in half the butter for 5 minutes. Transfer to a bowl with any liquid from the pan. Melt the remaining butter in the same pan and sauté the shallots until translucent. Add the thyme and wine and cook for 5 minutes. Set aside.

In a small bowl, whisk the cream with the egg yolk and mustard, stir in the mushrooms and then add the mixture to the shallots. Heat gently to warm the mushrooms through without boiling the sauce. Season with salt and freshly ground black pepper and sprinkle with the parsley. Serve immediately.

CARDONS A LA MOELLE

Cardoons with Beef Marrow

Cardoons are a delicate-tasting winter vegetable. Serve with roast turkey or chicken.

SERVES 4

1 cardoon
juice of 1 lemon
2tbsp plain flour
beef marrow bones from the butcher to
make 225g/8oz beef marrow
30g/1oz butter
2 shallots, finely chopped
150ml/5fl oz white Burgundy wine
200ml/7fl oz beef or vegetable stock
salt and freshly ground black pepper

Trim the cardoon, if necessary, by taking off the outer leaves, the thistles and the down.

Pour 1.1 l/2 pts of water and the lemon juice into a large saucepan. In a bowl, mix the flour with 3 tablespoons of water until smooth, then whisk into the saucepan.

Slice the cardoon stalks thickly, then place them in the saucepan. Cover and simmer for 1½ hours or until tender. Meanwhile, gently poach the marrow bones in simmering water for 1-2 minutes. Drain carefully and allow to cool slightly. Extract the marrow with a sharp knife or a teaspoon. Refresh the marrow gently in a bowl of cold water and dice it.

Melt the butter in a small saucepan, add the shallots and sauté until translucent. Add the wine and boil to reduce by half. Add the stock and simmer for 10 minutes. Season to taste.

Preheat the oven to 190°C/375°F/gas mark 5. Lightly grease an oven-proof serving dish.

Drain the cardoon, then transfer to the dish. Cover with the diced marrow and the sauce and bake for 10 minutes until golden.

POTEE DE LENTILLES DIJONNAISE

Thick Lentil Soup

In Dijon lentils are eaten with thick slices of pâté de campagne. This filling soup combines both ingredients.

SERVES 4

200g/7oz green lentils
1 onion studded with 1 clove
1 carrot, sliced
1 leek, sliced
1 celery stalk
2 black peppercorns, crushed
sprig of fresh thyme
115g/4oz bacon rashers, rinded
4 thick slices *pain de campagne*
2tbsp butter
120g/4½oz *pâté de campagne*
4tbsp crème fraîche
salt and freshly ground black pepper

Put the lentils, onion, carrot, leek, celery, peppercorns, thyme and bacon in a large saucepan with 900ml/1⅔pt of water and simmer, uncovered, for 30 minutes until the lentils are tender but still holding their shape.

Using a slotted spoon, remove the onion, thyme and celery from the pan and discard. Remove the rashers of bacon, dice them and return to the pan. Season with salt and freshly ground black pepper to taste.

Melt the butter in a frying pan and sauté the bread on both sides until golden. Drain well on paper towels. Divide the pâté between 4 individual soup plates or place in a tureen. Cover with the bread and pour the soup over. Place one tablespoonful of the crème fraîche on each plate or all the crème fraîche in the centre of the tureen. Serve immediately.

TRUITES AU VIN ROUGE

Trout cooked in Red Wine

At the twelfth-century abbey of Fontenay the monks created ponds and artifical bends in the river to raise fish such as trout. You can serve this dish cold in aspic, by stirring half a sachet of aspic into the hot sauce, pouring it over the trout, leaving to cool and chilling overnight.

SERVES 4

4 trout, 200g/7oz each, cleaned
750ml/27fl oz red Burgundy wine
2 onions, very finely chopped
2 carrots, sliced
1 bouquet garni
55g/2oz butter
3 shallots, finely chopped
1tbsp plain flour
salt and freshly ground black pepper

Preheat the oven to 220°C/425°F/gas mark 7.

Bring the wine to the boil in a flame-proof casserole with the onions, carrots and bouquet garni. Lower the heat and simmer, uncovered, for 5 minutes, then set aside to cool.

Butter an oven-proof dish and lay the trout side by side in the dish. Season with salt and freshly ground black pepper.

Pour over the wine mixture and bake for 10 minutes, basting the fish once with the wine.

Meanwhile, melt the butter in a saucepan, add the shallots and cook for 5 minutes until they are soft. Sprinkle in the flour and let the mixture bubble for 2-3 minutes, stirring.

Remove the trout from the oven and transfer to a serving dish. Cover and keep warm in the turned-off oven. Add the liquid from the fish to the shallot mixture and whisk. Bring to the boil, then simmer for 5 minutes, stirring all the time. Serve the trout covered with the sauce.

LE FRICOT DE CANARD AUX NAVETS

Duck Fricassee with Turnips

The traditional version of this recipe uses a whole duck. Nowadays, it is usually only the legs that are used to make the stew.

SERVES 4

**4 large duck legs, or 1 whole duck cut
into 8 pieces
20 pickling onions
55g/2oz butter
450g/1lb turnips, quartered
2tsp sugar
45g/1 ½ oz plain flour
300ml/10fl oz chicken or vegetable stock
250ml/8fl oz white Burgundy wine
2 garlic cloves, crushed
1 bouquet garni
salt and freshly ground black pepper
small bunch fresh parsley, finely chopped**

In a large flame-proof casserole, sauté the duck legs in their own fat for 20-25 minutes until browned. Take out the duck. Discard all but 2 tablespoons of the fat. Brown the onions in the remaining fat. Remove and set aside.

Melt the butter in the casserole, then sauté the turnips over a high heat for 1-2 minutes. Sprinkle with salt and cook for 1 minute or until golden. Add the sugar, lower the heat and cook for 2-3 minutes until the turnips have caramelized slightly. Remove and reserve.

Add the flour to the casserole and cook for 2-3 minutes, stirring. Stir in the stock, wine, garlic and bouquet garni. Return the duck to the casserole and simmer for 1 hour. Add the onions and turnips and cook for 15 minutes or until the meat is tender. Remove the bouquet garni and serve garnished with parsley.

POULET CRAPAUDINE

Spatchcock Poussins with Mustard

The flattened poussins in this dish are said to resemble toads or crapauds, hence the rather unusual title. If each poussin weighs under 450g/1lb, grill them for 5 minutes less at the beginning. The breadcrumbs form a crisp crust which keeps the meat juicy. You can vary the taste by using different varieties of mustard.

SERVES 4

**4 poussins or young chickens weighing
between 450g-675g/1-1 ½ lb each
30g/1oz butter, melted
1tbsp Dijon mustard
2tbsp fine breadcrumbs
juice of 1 lemon
salt and freshly ground black pepper**

Preheat the grill to high.

To spatchcock each poussin, first cut off the wing portions. Cut along each side of the backbone with poultry shears or kitchen scissors and remove it. Wipe the inside of the poussin clean with paper towels. Open the poussin out and snip the wishbone in half. Flatten the poussin by pressing down heavily on the breast to break the breastbone. Brush the poussin with butter and season.

Place under the grill for 15 minutes, skin side up. Turn over and brush with more butter and grill for a futher 10 minutes.

Remove the poussins from under the grill. Brush the skin sides with mustard and sprinkle with breadcrumbs.

Grill for 10 minutes longer or until the juices run clear (make sure the poussins do not brown too much). Sprinkle with lemon juice and serve with *Champignons à la Dijonnaise* (see page 84).

COQ AU VIN

Chicken with Red Wine Sauce

A classic Burgundian dish, this is found in different guises all over France. Make sure you use an older bird with more flavour. Use a robust wine, but not an expensive one, as the aromas of a subtle wine will be destroyed during the long cooking. (Illustrated opposite)

SERVES 4

**1.5kg/3 ½ lb free-range chicken, jointed
750ml/1 ⅓ pt red Burgundy wine
1 onion, sliced
2 carrots, sliced
1 leek, sliced
2 garlic cloves, crushed
2tbsp vegetable oil
30g/1oz butter
1 bouquet garni
200ml/7fl oz chicken stock
4tbsp marc or brandy
30g/1oz plain flour or arrowroot
salt and freshly ground black pepper**

FOR THE GARNISH

**200g/7oz streaky smoked bacon, rinded
and diced
20 small pickling onions
150g/5 ½ oz button mushrooms, trimmed
30g/1oz butter
2 slices of white bread, quartered
1 garlic clove, halved**

In a large saucepan, bring the wine to the boil and simmer for 5 minutes, then leave to cool.

Place the chicken together with the onion, carrots, leek, garlic and bouquet garni in a large non-metallic bowl, pour in the wine, then cover tightly with cling film and marinate overnight in the refrigerator.

Drain the chicken pieces and vegetables, reserving the marinade liquid. Pat the chicken dry with paper towels. Set aside the vegetables.

Sauté the chicken pieces in the oil and half the butter in a large flame-proof casserole for 5 minutes on each side. Drain off most of the fat, then add the vegetables. Sauté for 5 minutes, then add the reserved marinade liquid with the bouquet garni and enough of the stock to cover the chicken pieces. Simmer gently, covered, for 40 minutes or until the meat is tender and the juices run clear if the meat is pierced with the tip of a knife.

Meanwhile prepare the garnish. Sauté the bacon for 5 minutes in a frying pan. Add the onions and cook until browned, then add the mushrooms, and butter if necessary, and cook for 5 minutes. Remove the bacon, mushrooms and onions and set aside. Rub the bread with the garlic, then sauté in the same pan until browned. Add more butter if necessary. Remove from the pan and reserve.

When the meat is cooked, strain off the liquid into a saucepan. Discard the vegetables and bouquet garni. Add the marc to the saucepan and, over a medium heat, thicken with the flour, stirring constantly. Season to taste. Serve the chicken pieces covered with the sauce and garnished with the mushrooms, onions, bacon and sautéed bread triangles.

LAPIN A LA DIJONNAISE

Rabbit with Mustard

Rabbit and hare are still a very common sight in the countryside and farms throughout Burgundy. This traditional dish makes use of Dijon mustard, another speciality of the region. Mustard oils evaporate in heat, so mustard must always be added to a recipe at the very end of the cooking time. Once you have opened a jar of mustard, pour a little oil into the jar each time you use it to stop the mustard from drying out. (Illustrated above)

SERVES 4

1.5 kg/3 ¼ lb rabbit, cut into 8 pieces
750ml/27fl oz dry white wine
4tbsp white wine vinegar
2 onions, sliced
1 carrot, sliced
1 bouquet garni consisting of 1 sprig of thyme, 1 sprig of parsley, 1 bay leaf and 5 peppercorns, tied up in a muslin bag with string
1tsp sea salt
100g/3 ½ oz butter, softened
5tbsp strong Dijon mustard
8 streaky bacon rashers

100ml/3 ½ fl oz single cream
salt and freshly ground black pepper
1tbsp fresh chives, finely chopped,

The day before cooking, place the rabbit in a non-metallic bowl with the white wine, vinegar, onions, carrot, bouquet garni and sea salt, cover and leave for 2-3 hours or overnight in the refrigerator.

The next day, preheat the oven to 200°C/400°F/gas mark 6.

In a small bowl, mix half of the butter with half of the mustard until smooth. Take the rabbit pieces out of the marinade and pat dry with paper towels; reserve the marinade. Spread the butter and mustard mixture over the rabbit pieces, then wrap a bacon rasher round each piece. Place the pieces in a roasting tin and cook in the oven for 25-30 minutes or until they are tender and the juices run clear when the meat is pierced with the tip of a sharp knife. Baste with the reserved marinade if the pieces appear to be drying out while cooking.

Meanwhile, make the sauce. Pour the reserved marinade into a saucepan. Bring the marinade to the boil and then simmer for 10 minutes until slightly thickened and reduced.

When the rabbit is cooked, remove from the oven, transfer to a serving dish, cover and keep warm in the bottom of the turned-off oven. Remove the bouquet garni from the marinade and pour the marinade into the roasting tin. Simmer for 5 minutes, stirring to scrape up all the cooked bits from the bottom of the tin.

Stir the cream into the tin and simmer for a further 5 minutes. At the last minute, add the remaining butter and mustard to the sauce and whisk. Season to taste. Serve the rabbit pieces with the sauce spooned over the top and garnish with the chopped chives.

COTELETTES DE PORC SAUCE PIQUANTE AVEC OIGNONS AU VINAIGRE

Pork Chops in Wine Vinegar and Mustard with Pickled Onions

At the beginning of the twentieth century wine was scarce as phylloxera ravaged the vines. Since lemons were, as yet, unavailable, vinegar was often used to flavour food, as in this recipe. You can add more vinegar to the recipe if you prefer a sharp flavour.

SERVES 4
4 pork chops
1tbsp plain flour
30g/1oz butter
1 garlic clove, crushed
1 bouquet garni
4 shallots, finely chopped
1tbsp Dijon mustard
1tbsp white wine vinegar
6-8 gherkins, diced
salt and freshly ground black pepper

FOR THE PICKLED ONIONS
450g/1lb tomatoes
2 onions, chopped
3 garlic cloves
9tbsp olive oil
2-3 basil leaves, torn
1 bouquet garni
1kg/2¼lb pickling onions
100g/3½oz raisins
200ml/7oz white wine vinegar
85g/3oz sugar
salt and freshly ground black pepper

Prepare the onions a day ahead. Put the tomatoes, the chopped onions, garlic, 3 tablespoons of oil, the basil, bouquet garni and seasoning in a saucepan and simmer gently, covered, for 30 minutes.

Add the pickling onions, raisins, remaining olive oil, vinegar, sugar and seasoning to the saucepan. Pour in 500ml/16fl oz water and bring to the boil. Lower the heat and simmer gently, uncovered, for 1 hour. Leave to cool, then cover and refrigerate until needed.

The next day, place the flour and seasoning in a small bowl or saucer and dip each chop into the flour to coat it. Melt the butter in a large frying pan and sauté the chops, one by one, over a medium heat for 10-15 minutes until brown on both sides. Return all the chops to the pan, then stir in 250ml/8fl oz of water.

Add the garlic, the bouquet garni and season well. Simmer for 10 minutes, then stir in the shallots and simmer for a further 10 minutes, adding a little water if necessary.

Combine the mustard and vinegar, then sprinkle over the chops and add the gherkins. Cook for 3-4 minutes over a low heat. Transfer the chops to a serving dish, spooning the sauce over. Serve with the pickled onions.

JAMBON PERSILLE

Jellied Ham with Parsley

This dish is traditionally eaten at Easter and is made in a white earthenware or glass bowl. This recipe was given to me by Marie-Pierre Moine. It should be prepared the day before eating. Serve with mustard and gherkins.

SERVES 4-6
1kg/2¼lb uncooked ham or gammon, or a mixture of both

1 veal knuckle, cut into 2 pieces
1 calf's foot, split and blanched
2 beef marrow bones, chopped
(alternatively, substitute ½ sachet aspic for the above 3 ingredients)
1 onion
1 carrot
2 bunches of fresh parsley
2 sprigs each of fresh tarragon and thyme
1 bay leaf
8 black peppercorns
750ml/27fl oz dry white Burgundy wine
2tsp dried marjoram
1 sprig of fresh chervil, chopped
freshly ground black pepper

Put the ham in a large saucepan and cover with water. Bring to the boil, then drain and repeat twice, without draining the last time. Lower the heat and simmer for 30 minutes, skimming off any scum.

Drain the ham and leave to cool. Cut into chunks, discarding excess fat or tough rind. Return the meat to the pan. Add the knuckle, calf's foot and marrow bones if using, the onion, carrot, half the parsley and tarragon, all of the thyme, the bay leaf and peppercorns. Stir in 550ml/20fl oz of wine and add water to cover. Simmer gently for 1½ hours, covered, skimming off any scum. Season to taste.

Transfer the ham chunks to a bowl and set aside. Strain the liquid through a fine sieve into another bowl. Discard the sieve contents

If using aspic, soak it in the remaining wine for 5 minutes, then mix into the hot liquid. Season. Flake the ham with a fork. Chop the rest of the parsley and tarragon and add to the ham with the marjoram, chervil and some liquid.

Cover the bottom of a terrine dish with some of the liquid, then add a layer of the ham mixture. Continue layering, finishing with the liquid. Cool, then cover and chill overnight.

FLAMUSSE

Caramelized Pumpkin Cream

This recipe can also be made with pieces of apple. (Illustrated left)

SERVES 4
I small pumpkin, seeded and peeled to
make 450g/1lb flesh or two 225g/8oz tins
cooked pumpkin, drained
200g/7oz granulated sugar
3 eggs
150ml/5fl oz milk
1 sachet (7.5g/1⅔ tsp) vanilla sugar
1tsp ground cinnamon
30g/1oz plain flour

If using fresh pumpkin, coarsely chop the flesh, place in a large saucepan and cover with water. Bring to the boil, then simmer, without a lid, for 8-15 minutes until soft. Process the cooked or tinned pumpkin in a food processor or push through a sieve to make a purée.

Preheat the oven to 180°C/350°F/gas mark 4.

Make the caramel by gently heating half the sugar with a few drops of water in a small, heavy-based saucepan for about 5 minutes until the sugar colours. Transfer the caramel to 4 individual ramekins or one large 600ml/1pt mould, spreading it quickly around the base before it sets.

In a mixing bowl, beat the eggs, milk, remaining sugar, vanilla sugar, cinnamon and flour together. Add the pureéd pumpkin, beat well, then divide the mixture between the ramekins or pour it into the mould. Place the ramekins or mould into a roasting tin and pour in enough hot water to come half-way up the sides. Bake for 35 minutes or until a knife inserted in the centre comes out clean. Unmould and serve cold with whipped cream.

TROU BOURGUIGNON

Lemon Sorbet Perfumed with Marc de Bourgogne

This is usually served between courses to refresh the palate, hence its name, but it is also a delightful way to end a meal. As an alternative to this recipe, you can buy good-quality lemon sorbet, serve it in tall glasses, pour marc over the top and decorate with mint leaves.

SERVES 4-6
2tsp powdered gelatine
200g/7oz sugar
175ml/6fl oz lemon juice
finely grated zest of 1 lemon
2 egg whites
55ml/2fl oz marc or brandy
mint leaves, to decorate

Soak the gelatine in 4tbsp of cold water until softened, then stir to dissolve. Combine 170g/6oz of the sugar and 500ml/16fl oz of water in a small saucepan and stir to dissolve, then boil for 10 minutes to form a thick syrup. Take the pan off the heat and stir in the gelatine. Cover and leave to cool, then refrigerate for 1 hour.

Mix the lemon juice and zest into the syrup. In a small bowl, whisk the egg whites with the remaining 30g/1oz sugar until stiff, then fold them into the syrup mixture.

Pour the mixture into a freezer-proof container and freeze for 1-½ hours until the mixture is slushy. Whisk to prevent it from separating, then freeze for another 2 hours, whisking every 30 minutes until it thickens.

Stir in the marc and return the mixture to the freezer. Whisk once more before serving the sorbet in tall glasses, decorated with a few mint leaves.

PAIN D'EPICES

Honey Spice Bread

When I first arrived in Burgundy in the tiny village of Valfermet, my landlady, Madame Tilquin, prepared spice bread to welcome me. The main ingredients are honey and aniseed although there are many different variations. Some recipes call for honey alone, with no sugar, others specify the addition of orange and lemon peel. This recipe was given to me by Anne Willan and has the delicious fragrance of the pain d'épices *of my childhood. I have added ground ginger, but you can vary the spices. Buy whole aniseed and grind it in a pestle and mortar. (Illustrated right)*

MAKES 2 MEDIUM LOAVES
300ml/ ½ pt milk
450g/1lb honey
200g/7oz sugar
375g/13oz rye flour
200g/7oz plain flour
2 egg yolks, lightly beaten
2tsp aniseed, ground
½ tsp ground coriander
1tsp ground ginger
½ tsp ground cinnamon
½ tsp ground cloves
2tsp bicarbonate of soda
2tbsp chopped candied orange peel
(optional)
butter, for greasing

The day before baking, heat the milk, honey and sugar in a saucepan, stirring until the sugar dissolves. Bring almost to the boil, then remove from the heat and leave to cool.

Stir the rye and plain flours together in a bowl and make a well in the centre. Add three-quarters of the honey mixture and the

egg yolks to the well. Stir the mixture with a wooden spoon to gradually draw in the flour, then beat to make a thick, smooth mixture.

In a small bowl, mix together the spices, the bicarbonate of soda and candied peel, if using. Stir in the remaining honey mixture and add to the flour mixture, stirring until well combined. Cover with cling film and chill overnight.

Remove the dough from the refrigerator and bring back to room temperature. Preheat the oven to 160°F/325°C/gas mark 3.

Grease two 23x13x10cm/9x5x4in loaf tins and line with greaseproof paper. Spoon the mixture into the tins. Bake for 1 hour, or until a skewer inserted in the side of the bread comes out clean (it should not have shrunk from the sides and should be slightly soft in the centre). Leave until warm on a wire rack, then turn out to cool and peel off the greaseproof paper. The bread will keep for a month in a cake tin. Serve sliced and buttered.

HYPOCRAS

White Wine with Spices and Honey

The addition of spices and honey to wine was common practice in medieval times. This tradition is being revived by honey producers and others such as Madame Emorine of the Château de l'Aubespin. (Illustrated opposite, right)

FILLS TWO 750ML/1¼ PT BOTTLES
2l/3 ½ pt white Burgundy wine
125g/4oz honey
2 cloves
1 cinnamon stick
2 whole star anises
1 vanilla pod, slit and scraped

Mix the wine with the honey. Place 1 clove, ½ cinnamon stick, 1 star anise and ½ vanilla pod in each clean, dry bottle, then pour in the wine. Store in a cool, dark place for a few weeks.

GATEAU AUX RAISINS

Sultana Cake

This is a simple, traditional recipe, ideal as a special tea-time cake. (Illustrated opposite, left)

SERVES 8-10
85g/3oz sultanas
4tbsp marc or brandy
450g/1lb butter, softened, plus extra for greasing
450g/1lb sugar
6 eggs
600g/1¼ lb plain flour
2tsp baking powder
250ml/8fl oz milk
2tsp vanilla essence

Preheat the oven to 180°C/350°F/gas mark 4. Soak the sultanas in the marc for 1 hour in a non-metallic bowl. Grease a 23cm/9in loaf tin.

In a large bowl, beat the butter and sugar until light and fluffy. Add the eggs, one by one, beating well after each addition.

Sift one-third of the flour and the baking powder into the bowl, then mix in one-third of the milk and continue until all the flour and milk are used up. Stir in the vanilla essence. Remove the sultanas from the marc with a slotted spoon and fold them into the mixture.

Pour the mixture into the prepared tin and bake for 1 hour until a knife inserted into the centre comes out clean. Leave to cool in the tin on a wire rack, then turn out.

POIRES BELLES DIJONNAISES

Pears Poached in Red Wine with Crème de Cassis and Prunes

SERVES 4
4 Conference, Packham or Comice pears, peeled and left whole with stalks intact
500ml/16fl oz red Burgundy wine
3tbsp sugar
4tbsp crème de cassis
1 cinnamon stick
8 prunes, whole
85g/3oz flaked almonds, to decorate

Put the pears in a saucepan and pour in the wine, adding water to cover, if necessary. Add the sugar, crème de cassis, cinnamon and prunes and cook over a low heat, stirring until the sugar dissolves. Simmer for 15-20 minutes, stirring occasionally, until the pears are tender but still firm. Remove from the heat and leave the mixture to cool.

Meanwhile, toast the almond flakes in a dry frying pan for 3-4 minutes over a medium heat, stirring, until just golden. Turn out of the pan immediately, set aside and leave to cool.

Transfer the pears to a large serving bowl. Remove the cinnamon stick and pour the wine and prunes over the pears. Sprinkle with the almonds and serve with vanilla ice cream.

CREME DE CASSIS

Blackcurrant Liqueur

This delicious liqueur can be drunk either mixed with water or a chilled white wine such as Aligoté. This is a recipe from Madame Tilquin which was handed down to her from her grandmother, who was a distiller (bouilleur de cru).

MAKES 5L/8¾ PTS
2.5kg/5½ lb blackcurrants, unwashed
2.5l/4pt red Burgundy wine
sugar
75ml/5tbsp *eau de vie de prune* or vodka

Place the blackcurrants in a non-metallic bowl, pour over the wine and cover. Leave for a week in a cool, dark place, stirring a few times every day.

Crush the fruit in the bowl with the back of a spoon and press through a fine nylon sieve into a large, non-metallic bowl. Press through another finer sieve or a fine cloth suspended over a bowl.

Weigh the liquid and add the same weight of sugar, stirring until the sugar dissolves. Pour into a saucepan and bring to the boil, stirring all the time, then remove from the heat.

Stir in the *eau de vie*. Pour into warm, clean, dry bottles and seal. Store in a cool, dark place for 2 months and consume within 6 months.

LEFT *Fruits of the Clunisois preserved in marc.*
OPPOSITE *During the Middle Ages the abbey church of Cluny was the largest in Christendom. After the Revolution the town council sold it for building materials, but the soaring vaults that remain still convey some idea of its original grandeur. Chambertin, Meursault and Saint-Amour vineyards, among others, belonged to the abbey, as well as the whole town.*

TOP *A fisherman's view of the river Saône in the early morning. Amateurs and professionals alike fish the river for eels, bleak, crayfish, catfish, zander, pike and perch.*
ABOVE *Sunflowers are a common sight in summer.*
RIGHT *A view of Saint-Laurent on the river Saône facing Mâcon. Mâcon is a warm, sunny city with lively cafés and restaurants along the quais Lamartine and Boucheacourt, a market on the place aux Herbes and delicatessens and pastry shops along the rue Carnot.*

LA SAONE-ET-LOIRE

Southern Burgundy is made up of a number of distinctive *pays*, each one spectacular in its own way. These *pays* include Charolais, Brionnais, Clunisois, Mâconnais, Bresse Louhannaise and Côte Chalonnaise. It is a land of abundance, rich in the bounties of nature, and its heritage of great abbeys reflects its importance and wealth since the medieval period. Once the site of the largest church in Christendom, the abbey of Cluny, founded in 910, was the spiritual centre of Europe in the Middle Ages. In the thirteenth century over ten thousand monks in more than one thousand Benedictine abbeys throughout Europe took their orders from Cluny. The abbey itself was so vast that, during Pope Innocent's visit in 1245, it could house more than two thousand guests. The whole town belonged to the abbey, as did the neighbouring lands and vineyards. Between 1798 and 1823 the great abbey itself was almost entirely destroyed, and today one of the town's streets runs through what was once the central aisle of the monastery church. Though Cluny is now no more than a shadow of its former self, the spiritual life of the area lives on in such religious centres as Taizé and the Buddhist temple of Plaige near Toulon-sur-Arroux.

Leaving behind the gentle landscape of the Clunisois, the road crosses the flat-bottomed valley of the river Grosne before climbing up towards Chalon. Passing the Renaissance-style castle of Cormatin, one reaches the lovely medieval village and castle of Brancion high in the hills. The plains stretch out from Brancion towards Le Creusot and, to the east, the first of the vine-growing villages and domaines of the Côte Chalonnaise.

The main artery of southern Burgundy is the river Saône while the region's western reaches are bordered by the river Loire. In the picturesque towns of Chalon-sur-Saône and Tournus the houses are tall and slim, while in Mâcon brightly painted plasterwork suggests a hint of southern influence.

The Mâconnais is a region of vine-covered hills and stock-breeding meadows. As in Bresse, to the east, cereals, sugar beet, vegetables and poultry are the main products. South of Mâcon lies the Beaujolais, a land of high ridges, heavily wooded hilltops and vine-covered slopes running down to valleys threaded with streams. The wine of Beaujolais, unlike most other Burgundies, is best drunk young. Once almost exclusively produced as a cheap bar wine for the thirsty Lyonnais, it now has a wide appeal.

The cooking traditions of these regions have borrowed from each other over the centuries to produce one of the finest cuisines in the world. Many great chefs have trained in Lyon,

Vonnas or Roanne at such superlative establishments as Bocuse, Blanc and Troisgros. Here in this most southerly land, the wine tastes different, fruit and vegetables mature about three weeks before the rest of Burgundy, and the range of fresh produce is more varied.

Along the banks of the rivers Saône, Doubs and Seurre are restaurants seemingly unchanged since the turn of the century, which remind one of Impressionist images of Sundays on the river Seine. Here you can eat the specialities of the river: *friture de la Saône* (small fried fish), eels, *pochouse* (fish stew) and fried frogs' legs.

Across the Saône lies the distinctive region of Bresse, centred around the ancient salt port of Louhans on the rivers Seille and Solnan. The plain of Bresse is criss-crossed with rivers such as the Doubs and the Saône, and a network of ponds provide abundant fish. The land is flat, there is very little stone, and in the past the houses were built of mud and straw. Numerous old Bressan houses can still be seen along the small country roads, and most are still occupied. Tall chimneys – *sarrazins* – rise up from the roofs, and the hearth divides the central room in two. Food was cooked in a *crémaillère*, a pot hanging from a hook over the hearth. In French, *pendre la crémaillère* (hanging up the cooking pot) means to have a house-warming. On the outside, overhanging roofs provided shelter for drying out maize. Maize is still grown here and the cobs hang decoratively from the rafters of the houses. Indeed, the Bressans used to be known as *ventres jaunes* (yellow bellies) as their main diet consisted of a porridge of *gaudes* (a grilled maize flour similar to polenta). Both Bresse and the Charolais, to the west, specialize in raising beef, pork and poultry.

OF FLESH AND FOWL

The chickens raised in the region of Bresse are perhaps the most famous in the world, having the rare accolade of an *appellation d'origine contrôlée* (AOC). This applies to an area of three thousand five hundred square kilometres around Saint-Trivier-des-Courtes, and any Bresse chicken raised outside this territory has no right to the *appellation*. A ring on the left leg of each chicken shows the name and address of its breeder and a red, white and blue seal at the base of the neck names the person who reared it. The AOC label, from the Comité Interprofessionel des Volailles de Bresse (CIVB) indicates that the fowl is approved as being Bresse and states whether it is a chicken, a hen or a capon.

The chicks are hatched in only three hatcheries and sold on to farmers who raise them and sell them in turn to retailers. Bresse chickens are intentionally given insufficient feed so that they have to scrabble around for insects, snails and worms to supplement their diet. They are housed in wooden or plastic huts at night and are free to roam during the day.

Bresse chickens are, in fact, a semi-wild breed which would not fare well in battery ranges. There are about six hundred producers, many of whom raise only a few birds but others, such as Thierry Jalley, derive their livelihood from them. He and his wife Claire started raising Bresse chickens in 1985. At the time Thierry had five hectares, but this has now risen to fifty; it is important to have plenty of land, he explains, because the chickens eat tender young grass as well as wheat and corn.

TOP In the hamlet of La Mulatière near Mâcon, stands a typical Bressan house with its sarrazin *chimney. The chimney is set in the centre of the building over a hearth which once served for both heating and cooking.*

ABOVE *A fisherman returns from his early morning trip on a backwater close to Verduns-sur-le-Doubs.*
LEFT *La Grange-aux-Carrons is a fine example of a typical Bressan barn, its oak frame filled in with bricks and mortar and its overhanging roof covered with tiles.*

BRESSE CHICKENS

With their brilliant white feathers, delicate blue feet and very red crests with large crenellations, Bresse chickens are unmistakable. Brillat-Savarin, the nineteenth-century philosopher and native of southern Burgundy wrote: 'Chickens are to the kitchen what canvas is to the painter, or to charlatans the cap of Fortunatus: they are served up to us boiled, roasted, fried, hot or cold, whole or in pieces, with or without sauce, boned, skinned or stuffed and always with equal success.'

The best way to eat a Bresse chicken is either with a simple cream sauce or roasted (taking care to baste it often), so that the delicate taste of the meat is not lost.

Some of the great chefs of the area have devised special recipes for the Bresse chicken. At his restaurant near Lyon, Paul Bocuse cooks it in a large pumpkin and serves it with red Camargue rice and pumpkin gratin.

RIGHT ABOVE *A dish of* pochouse, *a stew traditionally made from local fish and acidic wine from the Noba grape, prepared at the Trois Maures, Verdun-sur-les-Doubs.*
RIGHT BELOW *Maize hanging to dry from the roof of a house near Saint-Germain-des-Bois.*

TOP ROW, RIGHT AND BELOW The Monday morning market at Louhans fills the Grande Rue and spills over into the place de Gaulle and the place Thibert. Dealers of clothes, goats' cheese, vegetables, fruit and garden herbs have traditionally been outnumbered by livestock traders, and especially by farmers of the distinctive white Bresse chickens.

Today, few people sell Bresse chickens at the market since most farmers sell directly to approved abbatoirs or butchers. However, there is a wide range of livestock for sale and the haggling involved before a deal is struck, makes this a noisy and entertaining event.

At any one time Thierry has approximately twelve thousand chickens. The chicks arrive a day old, weighing forty to fifty grams and venturing out only after fifteen days. They then spend five weeks outside, each chicken having about twenty square metres of terrain. A lovely scent of camomile pervades the air around the huts as the tiny chicks run about in the longer grass and scurry in and out of the huts. Each coop is moved to a fresh grassy spot when a new group of chickens arrives.

Once the chickens have reached saleable age they are removed from the fields and placed in wooden coops. They then spend between fifteen days and a month being fattened on a diet of corn, wheat, powdered milk and water. Male birds are at least four months old and hens five months old when sold, the latter having been fattened for a month. Capons, castrated at six to eight weeks, generally appear on the market at Christmas, when they are at least eight months old. The best place to sample Bresse chickens is at *fermes auberges*, such as Les Plattières at Sainte-Croix-en-Bresse or Groboz at Villemotier, where it is necessary to book in advance, or at the market café in Louhans on the day of the market.

LIVESTOCK MARKETS

The market in Louhans takes place on Monday mornings and starts with the arrival of the chicken dealers at about half past seven. Originally chiefly a cattle and pig market, it has now become a centre for the trade of Bresse chickens, but there are a few pigeons, rabbits, even the occasional goat and, at Christmas, the rare Bresse capons and turkeys. The larger part of the market, along the fifteenth- and sixteenth-century arcades of the square, has delectable vegetables, fruit, charcuterie, honey and goats' cheese. Sometimes there are lime tree leaves on sale; collected shortly after the trees have flowered in June, they make a soothing night-time drink after Burgundian indulgences.

The other important livestock market in southern Burgundy is that held every Thursday morning at Saint-Christophe in the Brionnais. This market specializes in the sale of Charolais cattle. The first written evidence of the market was found in a letter of 1488 from Charles VIII to Jean de Tenay of Saint-Christophe, giving him the right to hold three fairs a year for eternity. There are only thirty other cattle markets in France, of which this is the largest for Charolais. (The market at Moulins-Engelbert in the Morvan is smaller, selling only about three hundred head of cattle compared with the thousand or so traded every week at Saint-Christophe, and sales are by auction.)

The market at Saint-Christophe used to be held in the streets around the centre of the town which were unusually wide but, although ropes were put up to contain the animals, there were numerous complaints about the noise and the dirt. As a result the town hall bought the field which ran alongside the 'money wall' (where deals were made) at the turn of the century and built a covered enclosure ringed by metal bars. In a modern building in the middle of this enclosure the committee meets and the traders settle their contracts or discuss prices over the telephone. The sale of each category of beast – bulls, one-year-old grazers and calves – takes place at an allotted time every Thursday.

EMBOUCHEURS

The Charollais and the Brionnais regions border one another and developed complementary traditions as, respectively, breeders of cattle and embroucheurs (fatteners).

In the eighteenth century, farmers in the Brionnais became prosperous with the development of the market in Charolais cattle. Henri Velut (above) is an embroucheur from Saint-Christophe, one of the last of a fast-disappearing profession. He buys young cattle, raises them on his pasture land and sells them on. A good-sized animal in the peak of condition will weigh about eight hundred kilos and yield five hundred kilos of meat. Henri remembers one remarkable beast who weighed nine hundred and ninety-five kilos. She had a wonderful personality, came when she was called and allowed herself to be ridden by his children. Such a rare creature comes along once in a lifetime and Henri was disinclined to sell her until he had too good an offer to refuse. With regret, he took her to the abattoir and calmed her before she was stunned. He professes to be unemotional about his animals, although he evidently has a rapport with them: when he took me to see his herd, many of them approached him to be patted.

Charolais cattle are a distinctive and imposing breed, well known by now outside France. Pure white in colour, with white horns and pink nostrils, they have large eyes and foreheads, unusually long backs and a heavy frame. Pure Charolais cattle are registered and marked with an identification number and their feeding and living conditions are monitored: they must be kept outdoors and fed off the green pastures of the Brionnais or the Charollais. At the market animals are also checked against a register, and in butcher's shops this special organically produced meat is identified by means of a red Charolais label. The number of cattle in the market varies each week but during the summer there are usually about one thousand head, comprising bulls, bullocks, heifers and calves. Breeders, young and old alike, carry staffs and wear rubber boots and dark blue smocks reminiscent of the big peasant shirts of the past. The air is filled with the sound of bellowing cattle as buyers saunter among the stock, checking the size, height and weight of each animal: if it is heavily built, with well-rounded haunches, it will be sold very quickly. Once prices have been agreed, the animals are herded into a corral from which they will be led into the waiting trucks. This can be an anxious time for animals and human beings alike: often a bull will panic and charge in the wrong direction, to be chased by a buyer wielding his staff, while bystanders scatter. Trucks are lined up outside the stockyard, ready to take the animals back to the pastures or to the abbattoir.

The prices paid at the market form the basis for prices quoted for Charolais throughout France. The market is big business as the cattle can fetch very high prices. Twenty years ago, when beasts were bought for cash, an unsuccessful attempt was made to rob the local bank

TOP Charolais cattle being herded for loading. The Charolais breed was developed in the seventeenth century in the Arconce valley near Charolles. Initially reared as milking cows, they were later bred for their lean and tender meat. Now almost half the cattle in France are Charolais.
ABOVE Potential purchasers are experts in the finer points of flanks and haunches.
RIGHT AND FAR RIGHT The price for the week is set at a meeting held after the market closes. This price serves as an index for the whole of France.
OPPOSITE Charollais rams at the de Launay property outside Palinges.

on market day. Even in those days each beast was worth approximately eight thousand French francs – which would have netted the villains a tidy sum.

In the market café you are transported to timeless rural France. Men sit hunched over tables smoking, drinking coffee or wine, discussing prices and comparing their sales or purchases of the morning. A local speciality, *bouilli de Saint-Christophe*, similar to *potée bourguignonne*, is served in the café (see recipe on page 123). It dates back to a time when cattle were taken to market on foot the night before and a substantial meal was needed before the long journey home.

Charolais meat is tender and generally needs little preparation or cooking. It is best eaten as a *filet*, an *entrecôte* or a *pot au feu*. At La Fontaine in Châteauneuf (see page 112), we sampled a *filet* with a classic red wine sauce into which a dash of hazelnut oil (instead of butter) had been whisked at the end to give an extra tang to the sauce.

The Charollais offers an excellent breeding ground for sheep as well as cattle, and when French breeders went to England in the 1820s to select Durham bulls to improve the Charolais race, they also returned with Dishley rams from Leicestershire. These were then crossed with local breeds to produce the Charollais sheep of today. Some one hundred and forty years later François de Launay of Palinges saw their potential and started to breed them. They are sheep of unusual size and resistance: the ewes can weigh up to ninety kilos, while mature rams weigh as much as one hundred and thirty kilos. In the early 1960s there were twenty-four breeders of Charollais sheep in France; now there are two hundred and thirty. The rams are exported all over the world to be crossed with other breeds.

GOATS' CHEESE

At Saint-Denis-de-Vaux, in the heart of the Côte Chalonnaise, is the farm of Christian Donet, a man with a passion for goats. As a child, he dreamed of having goats and making goats' cheese and in 1991 his dream became reality. He is now president of the Producteurs de Fromages Caprins of Saône-et-Loire. Although goats' cheese is more difficult to age than cheese made from cows' milk, demand rises every year and the supply of goats' milk is steadily diminishing. Local goats' cheeses simply take the name of the village or the region where they are made. Each small, round Mâconnais cheese requires a litre of milk, whereas the larger, cylindrical Charollais uses two to three litres. Charollais goats' cheese is soon to be awarded an appellation d'origine contrôlée. *The goats are led to the fields in the spring and brought back to the farm in the autumn. They need a plentiful supply of fresh grass as a diet consisting entirely of hay gives goats' cheese a uniformity of flavour. Donet talks about his goats with such affection that he surprised me by saying that he makes delicious goats' sausage in the winter.*

OILS

Seemingly lost in the lush hills of the Brionnais is the tiny village of Iguerande, famous for its Romanesque church. Nearby is an old mill, l'Huilerie Leblanc, which makes the best oils in the region. Established in 1878 by the great-grandfather of the present director, Jean-Charles Leblanc, it sells oil to restaurants all over the world. Grilled rapeseed and walnut oils were most commonly used in cooking in the past. Now Leblanc makes these as well as olive and hazelnut oil, and has recently introduced pistachio nut and almond oils (right centre and right below). The nuts are ground slowly for twenty minutes using the mill's ancient granite stone (above). The resulting paste, which is more workable than that produced in an automatic mill, is lightly grilled and the oil is extracted by gentle pressing. The bottles are filled using special pumps (above right). Jean-Charles explained that the new tendency towards light meals with salads is a large factor in the continuing success of his business.

ABOVE Bernard Jacques pulling up crayfish baskets to check the catch.
TOP The Jacques family shake the bleak from nets pulled up at dawn from the river Saône. Bleak is served locally as petite friture.

GAME

Every Sunday morning during the hunting season the woods of the Charollais and the Brionnais resound with gunshots. The forests abound with game – deer, wild boar, hare and numerous species of birds – and it is not unusual to catch sight of boar or deer at dusk. At Easter in times past, the lord, or *châtelain*, of the manor would allow the local peasants to shoot hare on his lands. The eating of rabbit at Easter is perhaps a survival of this tradition.

Another traditional dish, often enjoyed after a successful hunt, is a stew made from the heart, lungs and liver of wild boar, cooked in red wine. It is washed down with celebratory draughts of red Burgundy. A similar stew, called *corée* or *fressure*, is made with the same parts of a lamb or pig on the day of its slaughter. Although traditional, these dishes would certainly not be to everyone's taste today.

While shooting remains the most common form of hunting, there are four liveried equestrian hunts in southern Burgundy. One of these is organized by Yves de Maigret, a breeder of Charolais cattle. He and his wife, together with between five and twenty-five companions, hunt twice a week during the season, which runs from September 15th to April 1st, chasing boar, fox and hare in the woods of the Charollais. For the larger animals they hunt with a pack of forty to sixty dogs, while for hare the pack is reduced to twenty. In November, on the feast of Saint Hubert, Yves de Maigret organizes a stag hunt for six or seven hundred riders, with correspondingly large numbers of dogs.

FROGS, FISH AND CRAYFISH

In the sleepy villages of southern Burgundy, one sometimes sees small boys with their fathers setting off early on Sunday mornings for a day's fishing in one of the picturesque rivers that criss-cross the region. Eyes trained on their floats, these Sunday fishermen sit with copious picnic lunches at their sides.

Up until the Second World War fishing was an important economic activity on the river Saône. Today there are fewer than thirty professional fishermen in southern Burgundy, and not many of these fish the Saône. One who does is Paul Buisson, who lives in the small village of Montbelay which, he maintains, is straight out of *Asterix*, the famous French comic books, because the village is a close-knit community where any occasion is good for a banquet. He used to fish the river Rhône but, because of increased pollution, abandoned it for the Saône. Every day at about four o'clock in the morning, he sets out to retrieve the nets which he placed the previous evening. The river, not fishing, is his passion, but he supplies zander, pike, carp and tench to the market at Lyon or to local restaurants.

Another local fisherman is Bernard Jacques, who is one of the few still to fish for crayfish. He fishes all year round in all kinds of weather, reaching his traps or nets before dawn, before any boats are likely to tangle or rip them. Smaller rivers such as the Doubs and the Seurre provide easier fishing grounds because there is less river traffic than on the larger rivers and, consequently, they are less polluted.

ABOVE *Paul Buisson returning with his catch.*
BELOW *Live fish being offloaded from the tank.*
BOTTOM *Bream, part of the day's catch.*

In the summer, depending on orders from restaurants or fishmongers, Bernard fishes small fish such as bleak, for the *petite friture de la Saône*. Bleak appear with the first rays of warm sun in the spring and he catches them in fine nets at dawn, takes them home to his backyard and disentangles them with the help of his nephew and wife. They clean the fish and then deliver them to the restaurants. The secret of the *petite friture* is to dip the fish in beer, then coat them in flour or *gaudes* (grilled maize flour) and deep fry them.

Having delivered the bleak, Bernard goes back to the river to pick up the crayfish. Despite the early hour, the sunflowers by the river banks are already beginning to bend their heads under the heat of the sun. The crayfish are caught in small wire cages baited with fresh fish, and are left in the river until required. The crayfish are eaten either with chicken or on their own; alternatively they form the basis of a *sauce Nantua*, which is served with *quenelles* (see recipes on pages 118-9). They are much in demand, and all year round Bernard sells as many as he catches; in fact he wishes he could find more. Some fishermen keep over one thousand cages in the river. He gestures around to the three or four other fishermen in boats nearby and laughs as he says, 'There is the rest of my family – my father, my uncle, my brother – we all have a passion for fishing.'

Frog-fishing is a mythical pastime associated in most French novels with childhood and, since Bresse is covered with a network of man-made ponds, I thought I might find a few fishermen. But frog-fishing in the wild is forbidden nowadays as French frogs are an endangered species. Most frogs' legs now eaten in France belong to the species *Rana rieuse*, and are imported from the old Eastern block countries and Turkey. They are fat and, connoisseurs say, not a patch on the flavour of the skinny French frogs (*Rana temporia* and *Rana esculanta*). Frogs are fished privately between July and October but cannot be sold.

In La Chapelle Saint-Sauveur, north of Louhans, I eventually came across Gilbert Morestin, the only man in Saône-et-Loire who raises frogs. There are only four authorized frog breeders in France, of whom two are in Burgundy. The ponds in which the frogs are raised are set among trees well away from cultivated fields (it was discovered that the frogs were dying as a result of contact with the fertilizers used to grow corn in Bresse). In the spring the frogs are placed in cement *bassins*, where they lay five hundred to three thousand eggs each. About ninety-five per cent of these will survive and reach adulthood in three years.

Gilbert Morestin also farms fish in thirty ponds, which cover about one hundred and fifty hectares. The interlocking ponds were probably built in the late Middle Ages, encouraged by the lack of tax on fish farming. In the sixteenth century parts of Bresse and the Dombes district were flooded to provide defences in the wars, but this brought malaria in its wake and, during the last century, life expectancy in the marshes was only twenty-four years. Many of the ponds were therefore drained, though some have been refilled this century.

There are numerous local methods of preparing river fish but the most celebrated dishes are the *matelote*, in which fish and eels are cooked with red wine, and the *pochouse*, a fish stew made with white wine (see recipe on page 118). Carp *filets* are served in a *sauce meurette* (see recipe on page 82). There are several restaurants, such as the Beaurivage in Chauvort and La Marine in Saint-Jean-de-Losne, at which local fish can be sampled, as can frogs' legs fried in butter with chopped parsley, garlic, lots of salt and white wine.

SALAD DAYS

A few years ago the area around Chalon was full of market gardens. Monsieur Maurice, who grows the finest herbs in the district, is soon to retire and the Friday market in the small square of Saint-Vincent in the centre of Chalon will no longer have a herb grower. However Madame Jeannine Putigny (left, above), whose family have had a market garden near Chalon for twenty-five years, will continue selling her produce there for some time to come. At a time when new and choice ingredients are a vital part of cooking, she supplies vegetables and berries to most star restaurants in the area; half a dozen chefs from Chalon and Beaune flock to her stall at half past six in the morning to snap up her best produce. The joy of her work and her outdoor life is apparent on her calm satisfied face. Her produce stands out in the market: crisp salad vegetables of all colours and varieties; large frisée which are covered with white plastic 'hats' while they are growing to keep the hearts white and tender (below right); plump yellow and red tomatoes; purslane; scented raspberries and fragrant melons. Her special pride is the growing of endives in the old-fashioned way, under a mound of earth to shield them from the sun.

ABOVE Nectarines displayed in the market at Louhans.
BELOW Liqueurs, spiced wines and digestifs, such as Suc Charolais, made to a nineteenth-century recipe at the Ducharne distillery in La Clayette, are a speciality of the region.

TOP CENTRE The Friday morning market on the place Saint-Vincent in Chalon.
TOP LEFT A beautiful display of courgette flowers.
ABOVE A narrow street in Cluny.
The tiles and slope of the roofs and the colour of the buildings and shutters indicate the influence of the south on this part of Burgundy.
RIGHT AND FAR RIGHT Local fruits, wild mushrooms in honey and vinegar, and scented vinegars prepared at the Château de l'Aubespin.

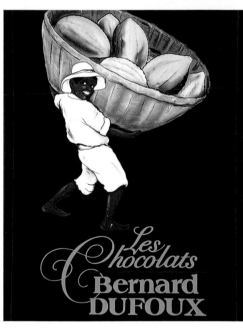

ABOVE AND TOP Many patisseries in the
region also make their own chocolates.
In La Clayette the master chocolatier, Bernard
Dufoux, makes some of the best chocolates
and cakes in France, including novelty
chocolates made with spices and marc.
Here, he can be seen holding a tray of fresh
chocolate palettes decorated with gold leaf.
His chocolate-making courses for beginners are
praised the world over.

SWEET DELIGHTS

One of the dishes most commonly eaten by Bressan families in the past was *gaudes* (a porridge made from grilled maize flour), which was served either savoury or sweet. It is no longer popular and few mills nowadays produce the maize flour to make it. One which does is the Moulin Taron at Chaussin, which makes a delicious stoneground nutty-flavoured flour. This was traditionally used to make crêpes (see recipe on pages 124-125). A thick version called *matafaim* (literally meaning 'tame your hunger') is remembered with pleasure by the older generation. Grilled maize flour is also used to make cakes and sablé biscuits.

After a visit to the market at Saint-Christophe it is well worth stopping at La Clayette, a small town with a fairytale castle with tall turrets which would not look out of place in a Disney cartoon. For gastronomes there is a wonderful surprise in store since the shop of one of the best chocolate makers in France is located here. Having trained under Maurice Bernachon, the famous chocolatier, in Lyon, Bernard Dufoux set up in business thirty-five years ago. He has two shops in La Clayette in which he sells chocolates, ice-creams, sorbets, *brioches aux praslines* and, once a year on August 15th (the feast day of the Assumption of the Virgin Mary), the traditional prune *brioches*. An imposing figure of a man, Dufoux claims that he eats at least four hundred grams of chocolate a day. He is a natural teacher and welcomes visitors to his kitchen, where he holds chocolate-cooking lessons every Wednesday. In the autumn he participates in '*la semaine du goût*', which takes place all over France, and is intended to introduce children to the subject of taste.

His cocoa beans come from Venezuela, Columbia or Ecuador and are highly perfumed. Once the pods have been roasted, the chocolate is extracted and melted, fresh cream is then added. Dufoux is currently experimenting with cinnamon chocolates and makes a 'chocolate foie gras' from chestnut purée, bitter chocolate and almond paste, which he suggests serving with a raspberry purée, a pistachio nut custard or a hot chocolate sauce.

Not far from Dufoux's shop is the small distillery of Vinauger du Charne, which opened at the back of a grocery store in 1855. It was bought a year ago by a young couple, the Ducharnes; the antique tools are still hanging on the walls and the oak vats are still in use. Fruit creams and syrups are prepared in the traditional way and the establishment is known for its old-fashioned liqueurs: *eau de noix*, made with green walnuts from the Brionnais, *liqueur de verveine* (verbena) and Suc Charolais, a bitter *digestif*.

Near Saint-André-le-Desert, north-west of Cluny, is the ruined thirteenth-century castle of Gros-Chigy, the childhood home of Marie-Louise Paccaud Emorine. Fired by the desire to create employment in the area, she is reviving traditional recipes, starting with jams from local fruit. She preserves fruit, such as *pêches des vignes* (vine peaches) in Marc de Bourgogne and makes aperitifs with peach leaves, wild cherries and a range of other fruit.

Everything Madame Paccaud Emorine sells is prepared by her and her produce makes wonderful presents. After only a few years of production she is being solicited by large companies to supply a range of preserves and other goods. One of the additional attractions of a visit to Gros-Chigy is a tour of the castle: the dungeons, the stable blocks and the old kitchen in the cellar, with its huge chimney, are fascinating.

WINES OF THE SOUTH

Differences in climate and the quality of the soil make the wines of southern Burgundy quite different in character from those of the north. An equally important influence on local wine production is the orientation of the vineyard slopes: while those of the Côte de Nuits and Beaune districts face east or south-east, those of the Beaujolais, Mâconnais and Côte Chalonnaise face south.

The vineyards of the southern *pays* make up seventy-three per cent of the total area of vineyards in Burgundy. The most concentrated area of vines is to be found in the Beaujolais – little is grown there other than vines – but vineyards also make up a significant proportion of the area around Mâcon and Chalon. In the past, most of southern Burgundy, much like the north, was covered by vines. Devastated by phylloxera and ravaged by two world wars, the areas which have been slow in replanting are suffering from depopulation and poverty while the Mâconnais and Beaujolais have regained their momentum through the vine.

From the Rock of Solutré, the famous escarpment jutting out from the plain of the Saône, and the flat lands of Bresse to the east, all one can see on the hillsides ahead, even on the steepest inclines, are the vines of the Pouilly-Fuissé and the Mâconnais.

ABOVE AND BELOW Vincent Joblot enthusiastically explains the nature and the joys of wine-making in the Clos Salomon, one of his vineyards on the Côte Chalonnaise. Joblot's premier cru Clos de la Servoisine is particularly highly regarded.

THE COTE CHALONNAISE

The wines of the Côte Chalonnaise have only recently been given an *appellation communale*. The wines are made from the two classic Burgundian grape types: Pinot Noir for the reds and Chardonnay for the whites. The landscape here is more varied than in the Beaujolais, as in between the vineyards there are meadows, orchards and market gardens.

Rully is a traditional centre of Crémant de Bourgogne, a sparkling white wine, and at Bouzeron you will find the best Bourgogne Aligoté, particularly at the domaine of Aubert de Villaine, co-director of Le Domaine de Romanée-Conti. Bouzeron will soon acquire an *appellation communale* of its own, with a corresponding rise in price.

DOMAINE JOBLOT

The vineyards just outside Givry have been blessed with excellent growing conditions and Vincent Joblot believes that, to maximize the earth's potential, you must respect it. He cuts his vines high, so that the grapes are aerated, and uses no chemical fertilizers. Pinot Noir is a difficult grape to grow so, in his view, holdings must be small if the vines are to receive the necessary care. Joblot stresses that if you want good wine you have to work for it.

The reds have aromas of vanilla and redcurrant, with a very long and well balanced flavour; they are wines to keep. The whites are delicate and very fruity. Since Joblot's production is small his stocks are usually sold out each year. This sometimes leads him to apportion the bottles for sale even before their release.

DOMAINE RENE BOURGEON

Near the town of Jambles, not far from Givry, the family of René Bourgeon have been producing wine since the 1530s. By 1969 they had only one hectare but, as a result of René's efforts, they now have a total of eight hectares. Through patience and sheer determination this self-taught man has won a number of awards for his wine including gold medals from fairs in Milan and Paris; these awards, together with newspaper articles in which his wines have been featured, cover the walls of his cellar where the intoxicating scent of the fermenting wine emanates from the oak casks.

A follower of the Steiner method of biodynamics, he explains that a mistake was made in the Côte Chalonnaise when the Bordelais method of wine-making was adopted in the 1970s. In the Bourgeon vineyard the grapes are hand-picked, vinified at a low temperature in open vats and mixed daily. Only natural grape yeast is used as each *terroir* has its own yeast which is a specific component of the wine it produces.

René's red Côte Chalonnaise, Givry and Givry *premier cru* La Barraude are some of the best Burgundian reds of the 1980s. The dark red wines have an elegant bouquet and a long finish, with aromas of red fruits: of blackcurrants and blackberries, cherries and raspberries. Although they are good now, they will be even better in ten years time and are still attractively priced.

ABOVE LEFT On a clear day, from the top of the Rock of Solutré, you can see across the vineyards of Mâcon and the Bresse to Mont Blanc.
ABOVE An unusual way of promoting local wines.
BELOW René Bourgeon produces premier cru La Barraude, a highly prized wine.

MARCEL LAPIERRE

At an old farmhouse outside Villié-Morgon, Marcel Lapierre (above left) produces some of the best Beaujolais and Morgon available. His family have made wine for three generations but, until recently, did not own the land. Now Lapierre has nine hectares of Morgon and one of Beaujolais. In 1978 he started to experiment with a cuvée grandpère *following traditional methods inspired by Jules Chauvet (one of the founding fathers of the return to traditional and organic wine-making). Marcel used no chemicals and even eschewed sulphur when bottling, to the surprise of all* viticulteurs. *After hand-picking and careful sorting, the grapes are left to ferment for one to three weeks without being crushed. The lowest grapes are crushed naturally by the weight above them, causing the juice to rise and fermentation to occur naturally. As far as possible, Lapierre avoids adding sugar. His wines are sold out from year to year, and in his own cellar he keeps little, leaving it for only a short time in the cask as wood obscures the fruity character of the Gamay grape. Pictured below are an assortment of rubber bungs (left) and wooden plugs (right) used for stopping casks.*

MACONNAIS WHITES AND REDS

The wines of the Mâconnais were mentioned by the Roman poet Ausonius, but it was the monks of Cluny who developed their cultivation. The predominant grape type in this southernmost area of Burgundy, where the climate is gentle and sunny, is the Gamay. To the west of the river Saône as far as Cluny and from Tournus southwards to Mâcon the landscape is hilly and soft, the vineyards alternating with meadows and fields. To the west of Mâcon, the hills become higher and rougher, dominated by vast crags such as the Rock of Solutré and Vergisson. Some of the best whites of Burgundy – Pouilly-Fuissé, Pouilly-Vincelles, Pouilly-Loche and Saint-Véran are grown on these harsh slopes.

The Mâcon white wines are fresh and supple and the reds earthy and simple, and best drunk young. Every year in May a wine fair is held in Mâcon, at which the wines of Burgundy are presented. As part of this fair a Concours National des Vins de France is organized at the Lycée Agricole of Mâcon Davayé. More than twelve thousand French wines are represented and tasted by one thousand two hundred tasters.

ABOVE A sculpture in Mâcon of two harvesters carrying grapes in the old-fashioned way. *BELOW The aromatic white wines of the Pouilly-Fuissé come from vineyards at the foot of the Rock of Solutré.*

JEAN-JACQUES VINCENT

The expertise of four generations of wine-making, a degree in oenology and a life devoted to imparting knowledge to others in his capacity as professor in the Lycée of Mâcon-Davayé make Jean-Jacques Vincent one of the best-informed as well as one of the finest makers of Pouilly white wines. He lives at Château Fuissé, which stands at the end of the village of Fuissé. The slopes of the surrounding Mâconnais hills are covered with vines of Chardonnay grapes, which grow right up to the walls of the chateau. The harvest of the Vincents' thirty hectares of vineyards is done entirely by hand; the grapes are picked whole and pressed immediately. The cellars contain row upon row of oak barrels where the wines mature. The *cuveries* are air-conditioned and the temperature of the wine vats is monitored daily.

His wines are pale yellow and pellucid, with an aroma of pears and hazelnuts. They are elegant wines with a strong personality and a long finish and they keep well. His special *cuvée* made from the fruit of old vines – those over sixty years old – is a delectable treat.

BELOW A sign at Chenas for Beaujolais illustrates the traditional means of transporting grapes.

THE BEAUJOLAIS

The journey from the Rock of Solutré south to the Beaujolais is a dramatic one. The road winds through steep-sided valleys and over mountain tops, and wherever one looks there are vines. Many of the houses are new or recently renovated, and betray the wealth that has come about from the vine in the Beaujolais.

North Beaujolais has a granite soil which suits the Gamay grape. The ten *crus* of the region, the *appellation communales* of Beaujolais, are northernmost while the Beaujolais-Villages and Beaujolais Supérieur, both *appellations régionales*, extend south towards Lyon.

LA FONTAINE

CHATEAUNEUF, TEL 85 26 26 87

After working for famous chefs such as Bocuse, La Mère Brazier, Léon de Lyon, Ledoyen and Michel Guérard, Jean-Yves Jury (left) returned to his origins in the tiny village of Châteauneuf in the Brionnais. Born in nearby Chaufailles, his grandmother was known as La Mère Gueneau at a time when the Lyonnais district was famous for its 'grandmères', women who ran family bistros offering traditional hearty home-cooking of the highest quality.

The Jurys bought La Fontaine in 1988. The restaurant's simple exterior does not prepare one for the mosaic-studded interior reminiscent of Gaudi. The food, by contrast, is remarkably reassuring. Jean-Yves' cooking is close to the style of the 'grandmères' in that he prepares local dishes using local produce, and his food is extremely good value.

TIMBALE D'ESCARGOTS AUX LARDONS ET A L'ESTRAGON

Snails in a Bacon and Tarragon Sauce

(Illustrated left)

SERVES 4
4 shallots, finely chopped
4 sprigs fresh tarragon, finely chopped
3tbsp white Burgundy wine
1tbsp single cream
150g/5 ½ oz butter
4 dozen tinned snails, drained
3 smoked bacon rashers, cut into lardons
1 tomato, skinned, seeded and diced
small bunch fresh chives, finely chopped

Simmer the shallots and tarragon with the wine for 3 minutes. Add the cream and the butter. Bring to the boil for 5 minutes, whisking vigorously. Add the snails, lower the heat and simmer for 2 minutes. Sauté the bacon, drain the fat and add the bacon to the snails. Transfer to a serving dish and decorate with the diced tomato and chopped chives.

TOURNEDOS DE LAPIN AUX MORILLES ET AUMONIERE DE CHOUX

Rabbit Tournedos with Morels, Cabbage Parcels and Stuffed Courgette Flowers

(Illustrated opposite)

SERVES 4
2 saddles of rabbit, boned
325g/11oz fresh morels
15g/ ½ oz butter
3tbsp white Burgundy wine
125ml/4fl oz veal stock

FOR THE CABBAGE PARCELS
1 Savoy cabbage
1 onion, finely chopped
200g/7oz smoked streaky bacon, rinded and diced
1 garlic clove, crushed
2 sprigs fresh thyme
1 bay leaf
2tbsp olive oil
salt and freshly ground black pepper

CREME BRULEE A LA REGLISSE AUX FRUITS

Liquorice-flavoured Caramelized Cream with Fresh Fruits

This recipe is a modern, innovative version of the traditional and well-loved crème brûlée. The addition of liquorice powder provides a subtle contrast of flavour to the creamy taste of the dessert.

SERVES 4

6 egg yolks
30g/1oz liquorice powder or
½ tsp vanilla essence
200g/7oz single cream
115g/4oz raspberries
115g/4oz redcurrants
1 grapefruit, peeled and quartered
1 kiwi fruit, peeled and quartered
3 apricots, peeled and quartered
200g/7oz strawberries, hulled and sliced
100g/3 ½ oz blackcurrants
55g/2oz brown sugar

In a heat-proof mixing bowl, beat the egg yolks with the liquorice powder or vanilla essence. Pour the cream into a saucepan and bring to the boil, then pour it over the egg yolks, stirring constantly. Return the mixture to the saucepan and heat it gently, still stirring, for about 2 minutes until thickened. Remove from the heat and leave the mixture to cool.

Distribute the fruits among four 7.5cm/3in ramekins. Preheat the grill to high. Spoon the cream mixture evenly over the fruit and sprinkle brown sugar over the top.

Place the ramekins under the hot grill for 1 minute or until the sugar has caramelized. Serve immediately.

FOR THE STUFFED COURGETTE FLOWERS
1 large courgette, sliced
1tbsp breadcrumbs
30g/1oz each cooked and uncooked ham
1 small bunch chives
100g/3 ½ oz butter
8 courgette flowers
salt and freshly ground black pepper

To prepare the cabbage parcels, blanch 8 of the outer cabbage leaves in boiling salted water for 4 minutes. Refresh under cold water and set aside. Remove the ribs from the rest of the cabbage. Shred the leaves.

In a frying pan, sauté the onion, bacon, garlic, thyme and bay leaf for 1 minute in 1 tablespoon of the olive oil. Add the shredded cabbage and sauté for a further 5 minutes. Season to taste. Place a tablespoon of the mixture in the centre of 4 blanched cabbage leaves. Bring the edges of the leaf upwards together to make a parcel. Tie the neck of each parcel with string and set aside .

To make the stuffing for the flowers, process the courgette, breadcrumbs, ham, chives and butter in the processor. Fill each courgette flower with the stuffing, place in a steamer with the parcels and steam for 10 minutes.

Lay each rabbit saddle on a blanched cabbage leaf and roll up with the leaf on the outside. Cover with cling film and cut into 2 slices (tournedos), without removing the film.

Sauté the tournedos and the morels in butter for 8-10 minutes. Take out the tournedos and the morels and deglaze the pan with the white wine. Simmer for 3-4 minutes, then add the stock and simmer for 2 minutes.

Peel the cling film away and present the tournedos and morels on a plate surrounded by the courgette flowers and cabbage parcels.

SALADE DE CHEVRE CHAUD

Salad with Grilled Goats' Cheese

This salad has now become a staple dish both in France and abroad. Demand for goats' cheese in the last few years has risen, and the *south of Burgundy is well placed as it is the largest producer of farmhouse goats' cheese. The cream dressing is versatile enough to be served with a variety of other salads. If you want a lighter salad, simply sprinkle walnut oil, sea salt, pepper and chives on each salad, omitting the cream, mustard and vinegar. Serve this salad as a starter or as a cheese course. (Illustrated above)*

SERVES 4

4 slices of *pain de campagne* or rye bread

4 small round dried goats' cheeses, each sliced in half to make 8 flat discs

450g/1lb mixed lettuce leaves, such as oak leaf, cos, lambs' lettuce or escarole

small bunch fresh chives, finely chopped

FOR THE DRESSING
150ml/5fl oz single cream
1tsp Dijon mustard
3tbsp sherry vinegar
3tbsp walnut or hazelnut oil
sea salt and freshly ground black pepper

To make the dressing, put all the ingredients in a bowl and whisk together. Season to taste.

Preheat the grill to medium.

Cover each bread slice with 2 slices of goats' cheese. Place the bread under the grill for a few minutes, or until the cheese has melted and turned a light caramel colour. Meanwhile, divide the mixed salad between four plates. Sprinkle the dressing over the top.

Place the grilled bread and cheese on top of the individual salads, sprinkle with chives and serve immediately.

GATEAU DE FOIES DE VOLAILLE

Warm Chicken Liver Mousse with Tomato and Basil Sauce

This dish originates from Bresse, and is supposed to be made with Bresse chicken livers, but use normal chicken livers if you cannot find them. In Bresse this is served with Sauce Nantua *(see page 119).*

SERVES 4
225g/8oz chicken livers, well trimmed with
any green spots cut away
1 garlic clove
1tbsp plain flour
3 eggs
3 egg yolks
1tbsp dry sherry

350ml/12fl oz milk
½ tsp ground coriander
salt and freshly ground white pepper
1tsp olive oil, for frying

FOR THE TOMATO COULIS
300g/10½ oz tomatoes, peeled, seeded and
finely chopped
1tbsp olive oil
8 fresh basil leaves, torn
salt and freshly ground black pepper

Preheat the oven to 160°C/325°F/gas mark 3.

Butter four 125ml/4fl oz ramekins, then line the bases and sides with greaseproof paper.

If your tomatoes are of good quality, make a cold coulis. Put the tomatoes in a bowl and mix in the oil and the basil and season to taste. Leave to stand while you prepare the mousse.

To make a warm coulis, place the tomatoes and the oil in a saucepan and simmer over a gentle heat for 20 minutes until reduced. Season with salt and pepper. Add the basil just before serving.

Coarsely chop the chicken livers and process with the garlic in a food processor. Add the flour, eggs, egg yolks, sherry, milk, coriander and seasoning and process again. To check the seasoning, heat the oil in a small frying pan and add 1 teaspoon of the chicken mixture. Adjust the seasoning if necessary.

Pour the mixture into the ramekins, then place in a roasting tin. Add enough hot water to come half-way up the sides of the ramekins.

Place the tin in the oven and cook for 25-30 minutes, or until a knife inserted in the centre comes out clean.

Remove the ramekins from the oven and leave to stand for about 2 minutes. Invert each mousse on to a plate, then lift off the ramekin and peel off the greaseproof paper. Spoon the tomato coulis around each mousse.

RILLETTES DE POULE

Chicken Rillettes

A typical Bressan version of rillettes made with chicken rather than the more traditional pork. These rillettes have a lovely flavour and are not at all fatty. They will keep for up to one week in the refrigerator. Serve with green salad and fresh, crusty country bread.

SERVES 10 AS A STARTER
450g/1lb back bacon
2kg/4½ lb chicken, cut into 8 pieces
350ml/12fl oz white Burgundy wine
3 sprigs of fresh thyme
1 bay leaf
75g/2½ oz goose or duck fat
45g/1½ oz lard, melted
salt and freshly ground black pepper

Cut the rind off the bacon and reserve, then cut the bacon into small pieces. Put the chicken pieces, bacon, bacon rind, white wine, thyme, bay leaf, a small amount of salt and pepper and 400ml/14fl oz of water to cover into a large flame-proof casserole.

Bring to the boil, skimming off all the scum as it rises, then cover and simmer gently for 3½ hours. Add the goose or duck fat and simmer, still covered, for a further 30 minutes.

Strain the mixture into a bowl, then return the liquid to the pan and boil to reduce by half. Leave the contents of the sieve to cool. Take out the chicken pieces and the bacon, remove the skin and the bones from the chicken and reserve the meat.

Take the liquid off the heat, add the bacon and chicken and mash with a fork. Adjust the seasoning and leave to cool. Pour into several small terrines or 1 large one and cover with melted lard to form a seal. Chill before serving.

TERRINE DE POULET AUX HERBES

Chicken Terrine with Herbs

Serve this terrine as a starter with pickled onions and gherkins, or as a main course with a mixed salad. (Illustrated left)

SERVES 6 AS A STARTER
8 rashers bacon
3 fresh sage leaves
200g/7oz boneless veal shoulder
150g/5 ½ oz back bacon, rinded
125g/4 ½ oz uncooked ham
75ml/2½ fl oz single cream
1 egg
1tbsp marc or brandy
2 small bunches fresh parsley,
finely chopped
3 sprigs fresh tarragon, finely chopped
1 small bunch fresh chives, finely chopped
2 chicken breasts and 2 chicken legs,
boned, skinned and cut into strips 15cm/6in
long and 1cm/½ in thick
salt and freshly ground black pepper

Preheat the oven to 200°C/400°F/gas mark 6.

Line a deep 20cm/8in oven-proof terrine with 5 bacon rashers and the sage leaves, overlapping them to make a lattice pattern.

In a food processor, mince the veal, the back bacon and half the ham. Cut the remaining ham into small cubes. In a small bowl mix the cream with the egg, marc or brandy, herbs, salt and pepper, then add the minced meat. If the ham is already very salty be careful not to add too much salt.

To check the seasoning, quickly fry a teaspoon of the mixture in a small frying pan and taste. Adjust the seasoning if necessary.

Cover the bacon rashers with a layer of the

meat mixture, then a layer of chicken, then cubed ham. Continue layering, ending with the meat mixture and remaining bacon rashers.

Place the terrine in a roasting tin and pour in enough water to come halfway up the sides. Cook for 1 hour until the meat has completely shrunk away from the sides. Remove from the oven and leave to cool, then cover and chill for at least 12 hours.

SOUFFLE AUX POIREAUX

Leek soufflé

This delicate soufflé is a variation on the traditional Burgundian leek tart or flamiche.

SERVES 4

45g/1 ½ oz butter, plus extra for greasing
2tbsp breadcrumbs
3tbsp plain flour
150ml/5fl oz vegetable stock
100ml/3 ½ fl oz crème fraîche
1 small onion
½ bay leaf
pinch of grated nutmeg
250g/8oz leek whites, finely chopped
3 eggs, separated
3tbsp grated Comté or cheddar cheese
salt and freshly ground pepper

Preheat the oven to 180°C/350°F/gas mark 4.

Lightly butter a 20cm/8in soufflé dish. Coat the inside of the dish with the breadcrumbs.

Melt 45g/1 ½ oz butter in a small saucepan placed over a large saucepan of simmering water. Stir in the flour and cook for 5 minutes, stirring constantly, without browning the mixture. Slowly whisk in the stock and crème fraîche, then add the onion, bay leaf and

nutmeg and cook for 30 minutes or until the sauce has thickened, stirring from time to time.

Meanwhile, melt the remaining butter in a saucepan, add the leeks, cover and cook for about 10 minutes or until they are soft.

Remove the onion and bay leaf from the sauce. Stir in the leeks, lower the heat, add the egg yolks and cook for 3-4 minutes, stirring constantly. Mix in the cheese and seasoning.

Allow the leek mixture to cool, then beat the egg whites until stiff peaks form. Gently fold the whites into the mixture, then spoon into the prepared soufflé dish and bake for 40 minutes or until well risen. Serve immediately.

PUREE DE CELERI

Celeriac Purée

This purée is delicious served with lamb dishes such as Sliced Leg of Charollais Lamb (see page 121).(Illustrated on page 121, left)

SERVES 4

400g/14oz celeriac, peeled and chopped
150g/5 ½ oz potatoes, chopped
1 garlic clove
55g/2oz butter
salt and freshly ground black pepper
1 small bunch fresh parsley, finely chopped, to garnish

Place the vegetables and the garlic clove in a saucepan and add salted water to cover. Bring to the boil and cook for 10 minutes or until tender. Drain the vegetables and garlic clove, then purée them through a sieve or in a food processor and add the butter. Season to taste with salt and freshly ground black pepper, garnish with the chopped parsley and serve immediately.

PUREE DE MARRONS

Chestnut Purée

Serve this purée with lamb (see page 121) or game. You can buy the chestnut purée in tins from most larger supermarkets. (Illustrated on page 121, right)

SERVES 4

300g/10½ oz potatoes, peeled and chopped
300g/10½ oz unsweetened chestnut purée
115g/4oz butter
85ml/3fl oz single cream
3tbsp marc or brandy
salt and freshly ground black pepper

Place the potatoes in a saucepan, cover with salted water and boil for about 15 minutes until tender, then drain well. Transfer the potatoes to a large bowl and mash them well, gradually adding all the other ingredients. Season to taste with salt and freshly ground black pepper.

Serve immediately or set the bowl inside another bowl of hot water to keep warm.

POCHOUSE DE VERDUN

Freshwater Fish Stew

This stew originated in Verdun-sur-les-Doubs in the seventeenth century when woodcutters, who floated the timber from the Jura on the Doubs, would prepare a fish stew using local wine. This was made from Noha, a very acidic grape variety, which has since disappeared. The name of the dish comes from the local word for fisherman. La confrérie de la Pochouse, *established in Verdun in 1949, fiercely protects the origins of the* dish.

Substitute bream for carp, lemon sole or plaice for perch, and hake or whiting for pike. The more acidic the wine you use, the better.

SERVES 4-6
2kg/4½ lb mixed freshwater fish such as carp, perch, pike and eel, cut into thick steaks
225g/8oz butter
2tbsp vegetable oil
4 shallots, finely chopped
750ml/27fl oz dry white wine, such as Aligoté
150g/5 ½ oz crème fraîche
1 garlic clove, halved
4 slices of white bread
8 sprigs fresh chervil or fresh parsley, finely chopped, to garnish
salt and freshly ground black pepper

Gently poach the pieces of fish for 5 minutes in a 400ml/14fl oz of water with 30g/1oz of the butter and the oil.

Remove the fish from the poaching liquid, transfer to a serving dish and keep warm. Skim any fat from the surface.

Melt 30g/1oz of the butter in a large saucepan or flame-proof casserole and sauté the shallots until they are translucent. Add the white wine and the poaching liquid and bring to the boil to reduce by three-quarters. Whisk in the crème fraîche and, at the last minute, whisk in 150g/5 ½ oz of the butter, cut into pieces. Season to taste.

To make the croutons, rub garlic on the bread slices, then cut into cubes. Melt the remaining butter in a frying pan, add the bread and fry until golden and crisp on both sides. Drain well on paper towels.

Pour the sauce over the pieces of fish, then sprinkle with chopped chervil or parsley, arrange the croutons on top and serve.

QUENELLES DE BROCHET AVEC SAUCE NANTUA

Quenelles with Crayfish Sauce

This dish is often found ready-prepared in French delicatessens. Any full-flavoured fish, such as whiting or even salmon can be subsituted for the pike. If you ask your fishmonger to fillet the fish, be sure to ask for the skin, bones and head because they are needed for the Sauce Nantua *(see page 119). (Illustrated opposite)*

SERVES 4-6 (24 QUENELLES)
550g/1 ¼ lb pike fillets, skinned
a half quantity of choux pastry dough (see page 30), omitting the cheese
Sauce Nantua (see page 119)
6 egg whites
500ml/16fl oz double cream or crème fraîche
pinch of freshly grated nutmeg
salt and freshly ground black pepper

Place the fish fillets in the food processor and purée them. Press the mixture through a fine metal sieve into a bowl. Cover and chill for at least 1 hour.

Meanwhile, prepare the half quantity of choux pastry dough.

When you are ready to make the quenelles, set the bowl of fish purée in a bowl of ice and water. Lightly beat 6 egg whites and work them slowly into the fish purée. Beat in the choux pastry dough, a little at a time. Gradually beat in the cream or crème fraîche nutmeg salt and pepper to taste. (Alternatively, process these ingredients together in a food processor and refrigerate the mixture for 30 minutes.)

Preheat the oven to 200°C/400°F/gas mark 6 and lightly butter an oven-proof dish.

Dip 2 tablespoons in a bowl of cold water. Scoop up a large spoonful of the mixture with 1 spoon, then use the back of the second spoon to smooth down the sides. Pass the mixture between the spoons, smoothing the sides until it is shaped liked an elongated egg.

Drop the first quenelle into simmering water and poach it for 2-4 minutes. If the quenelle falls apart, beat another egg white into the mixture and chill thoroughly. Shape the rest of the mixture into quenelles. Add enough quenelles to the pan to fill it without overcrowding and poach them for 15 minutes until firm. Dip the spoons back in the water before making the next quenelle.

Lift the quenelles out with a slotted spoon, drain on paper towels and arrange in a buttered oven-proof dish.

Preheat the grill to medium high. Bake the quenelles for 5-10 minutes in the oven until slightly risen. Cover with the *Sauce Nantua*. Place under the grill for 1-2 minutes to lightly brown the top. Garnish with the crayfish reserved from the *Sauce Nantua*.

SAUCE NANTUA

Crayfish Sauce

SERVES 4
115g/4oz butter
2 shallots, finely chopped
1 carrot, finely chopped
550g/1 ¼ lb crayfish
2tbsp marc or brandy
100ml/3 ½ fl oz white Burgundy wine
850ml/1 ½ pt fish stock
1 bouquet garni
45g/1 ½ oz plain flour
200ml/7fl oz double cream or crème fraîche
1tsp tomato purée (optional)
pinch of cayenne pepper
salt and freshly ground black pepper

Melt 1 tablespoon of the butter in a large saucepan. Sauté the shallots and carrot until they are soft. Raise the heat, add the whole crayfish and sauté for about 2 minutes until they just turn red. Add the brandy and flame.

Add the white wine, fish stock, bouquet garni, salt and pepper and simmer for 8-10 minutes until the crayfish turn bright red. Shell the crayfish, removing the intestinal vein and reserving the shells. Set aside until serving.

Process the shells in a food processor with a little liquid from the pan, until they are finely crushed. Return to the pan and simmer for 10 minutes. Strain through a fine sieve.

Melt the remaining butter in a saucepan, then whisk in the flour and cook, constantly stirring, for 5 minutes, or until foaming. Whisk in the shellfish liquid and bring the sauce to the boil, stirring constantly until it thickens.

Simmer for 10-15 minutes or until the sauce just coats the back of a spoon. Stir in the cream and bring just back to the boil. Add the tomato purée and season to taste.

POULET DE BRESSE A LA CREME

Bresse Chicken with Cream

Bresse chicken is reputed to be the finest-flavoured chicken in the world and, despite its price, it is worth trying at least once. This recipe was given to me by Claire Jalley, whose husband Thierry raises Bresse chickens (see page 96).

SERVES 4

1.7kg/4lb Bresse chicken or good quality free-range chicken, cut into 8 pieces
30g/2oz butter
3 onions, finely chopped
250ml/8fl oz white Burgundy wine
1 egg yolk
250ml/8fl oz crème fraîche
1tbsp lemon juice
salt and freshly ground black pepper

Melt the butter in a large flame-proof casserole and sauté the chicken with the onions until golden. Season with salt and pepper. Pour in the white wine.

Cover the casserole and cook over a very low heat for 30 minutes or until the chicken is cooked through and the juices run clear if the meat is pierced with the tip of a sharp knife.

In a small bowl, beat the egg yolk with 3 tablespoons of the crème fraîche.

Take the casserole off the heat. Transfer the chicken to a serving dish, cover and set aside.

Pour the remaining crème fraîche and lemon juice into the casserole, stirring all the time, then add the egg yolk mixture. Keep stirring over a low heat until the sauce thickens, taking care not to over-heat.

Spoon the sauce over the chicken and serve with a potato gratin (see page 31) or fresh pasta.

POULET DE BRESSE COCOTTE A L'ESTRAGON

Bresse Chicken with Tarragon

SERVES 4

1.7 kg/4lb Bresse chicken or good-quality free-range chicken, cut into 8 pieces
150g/5 ½ oz butter
5 small onions, finely chopped
5 shallots, finely chopped
3 garlic cloves, unpeeled
3 carrots, roughly chopped
6 sprigs fresh tarragon
100ml/3 ½ fl oz tarragon-flavoured wine vinegar
200ml/7fl oz chicken stock or water
1tsp Dijon mustard
2tsp plain flour
1tbsp tomato purée
500ml/16fl oz single cream
225g/8oz tomatoes, skinned, seeded and chopped
salt and freshly ground black pepper

Preheat the oven to 200°C/400°F/gas mark 6.

Melt the butter in a flame-proof casserole and add the chicken pieces. Sauté for 3-4 minutes until lightly browned. Season with salt and pepper. Add the onions, shallots, garlic, carrots and 4 sprigs of tarragon. Cover and cook in the oven for 30-45 minutes until the juices run clear when the meat is pierced with the tip of a sharp knife. After 15 minutes, moisten the chicken with 1 tablespoon of vinegar. Make sure the casserole does not become dry. When the chicken is cooked, transfer to a serving dish, cover and keep warm.

To make the sauce, deglaze the casserole by putting it over a high heat, adding 1 tablespoon of vinegar and scraping well. Add the stock and remaining vinegar and simmer for 3-4

minutes until reduced. Combine the mustard, flour and tomato purée in a bowl, then whisk into the stock along with the cream. Simmer for 5 minutes, then pass the sauce through a sieve into a bowl, discarding the sieve contents. Add the tomatoes and season.

Spoon the sauce over the chicken and garnish with the remaining tarragon. Serve with rice or fresh pasta.

JAMBONNEAU AU MACON

Braised Ham with White Wine and Vegetables

SERVES 4

900g/2lb ham hock or leg
500g/1lb leek whites
2 carrots
1 celery stick
1 garlic clove
115g/4oz shallots
1 bouquet garni
600ml/21fl oz dry white Burgundy wine, such as Mâcon
115g/4oz butter
200ml/7fl oz single cream
1tbsp Dijon mustard
salt and freshly ground black pepper

Put the ham hocks in a large saucepan, cover with cold water and bring to the boil, then drain. Repeat twice more.

In a food processor process the leek whites, carrots, celery, garlic and one third of the shallots until very finely chopped. Put the chopped vegetables, bouquet garni and wine into a large flame-proof casserole and bring to the boil. Add the ham, cover and simmer for 2 hours until the meat is tender. Halfway through cooking, turn the ham over and adjust the seasoning if necessary.

Make the sauce 20 minutes before the end of cooking. Sauté the remaining shallots in 30g/1oz of the butter for 5 minutes in a small saucepan. Ladle half the liquid from the ham into the saucepan, add the cream and mustard, and simmer for 3-4 minutes to reduce. Season and whisk in the remaining butter. Transfer the ham to a serving dish and slice it parallel to the bone. Serve with the sauce spooned over.

TRANCHE DE GIGOT DE MOUTON CHAROLLAIS AU VIN DE BOURGOGNE

Sliced Leg of Charollais Lamb in Red Burgundy Wine
(Illustrated right)

SERVES 4
1.35kg/3lb leg of Charollais or good quality
organic lamb, boned and cut into 4 slices
30g/1oz butter
1tbsp plain flour
1tbsp red wine vinegar
250ml/8fl oz single cream
salt and freshly ground black pepper

FOR THE MARINADE
750 ml/27fl oz red Burgundy wine
2 carrots, diced
2 onions, coarsely chopped
2 shallots, coarsely chopped
bouquet garni consisting of 2 garlic cloves,
2 cloves, 5 juniper berries and 5 black
peppercorns, tied up in a square of muslin

The day before cooking place the lamb in a non-metallic bowl and add all the marinade ingredients. Cover and chill overnight.

The next day strain off the marinade and reserve all ingredients. Pat the lamb dry with paper towels. To make the sauce, sauté the vegetables in 1 tablespoon of the butter for 1-2 minutes in a flame-proof casserole, then add the flour and cook for 5 minutes, stirring. Add the reserved liquid and the bouquet garni and simmer for 1 hour, uncovered, until the liquid reduces by three-quarters. Strain off and reserve the liquid. Discard the bouquet garni.

If you wish to thicken the sauce, purée the strained vegetables and add to the liquid.

Melt the remaining butter in the casserole and sauté the lamb slices for 5 minutes on each side until pink, or longer if you prefer the lamb well done. Add the vinegar to deglaze the casserole, scraping the bottom well. Stir in the cream and the sauce and season to taste.

Serve the lamb and sauce with Chestnut Purée and Celeriac Purée (see page 117).

BOEUF BOURGUIGNON

Classic Beef Stew

In Burgundy, beef was traditionally cooked whole with bacon. This stew has evolved from those days. The beef tenderizes beautifully in the red wine marinade and improves if kept for a short time, so you can make this dish in advance. (Illustrated left)

SERVES 4
1kg/2 ¼ lb leg of beef, cut into
85g/3oz pieces
400g/14oz carrots
200g/7oz back bacon, rinded and
cut into lardons
2tbsp olive oil
1 onion, sliced
1tbsp plain flour
6 garlic cloves
1 bouquet garni with the addition of 2 leek
greens and 1 celery stick
1tbsp marc or brandy
chicken stock, to cover
20 pickling onions
45g/2oz butter
200g/7oz button mushrooms, wiped
juice of 1 lemon
4-6 slices of bread to make croutons
salt and freshly ground black pepper
1 large bunch of parsley, finely chopped

FOR THE MARINADE
1 onion, finely sliced
3 garlic cloves, crushed
1 small bunch of fresh parsley
1 bay leaf
4 sprigs dried thyme
750ml/27fl oz red Burgundy wine
2tbsp olive oil
5 black peppercorns, crushed

The day before cooking, place all the marinade ingredients in a large non-metallic bowl, add the beef and cover tightly with foil. Refrigerate overnight, stirring 2 or 3 times.

Start preparing 3½-4 hours before you wish to serve. Coarsely chop 250g/8oz of the carrots. Over a medium heat, sauté the bacon in the oil in a frying pan until crisp. Remove with a slotted spoon and set aside Add the onion and chopped carrots and sauté in the bacon fat until lightly coloured. Strain the vegetables through a sieve placed over a bowl and set aside. Return the fat to the pan.

Remove the beef from the marinade with a slotted spoon and pat the pieces dry with paper towels. Place the flour on a saucer and season with salt and pepper. Dip each piece of beef in the flour and sauté them in batches over a high heat for 3-4 minutes each until they are nicely browned.

Strain the marinade, reserving the liquid. Transfer the beef to a flame-proof casserole and add the reserved liquid, the sautéed bacon, onion, carrots, 5 garlic cloves and bouquet garni. Flame the marc and add to the casserole. Add enough chicken stock to cover, then bring to the boil, cover and simmer gently for 2½ hours until the beef is tender but still firm. Skim off any fat from the surface.

Meanwhile, prepare the garnish. Sauté the pickling onions in 15g/½oz of the butter until just tender, remove and set aside. Slice the remaining carrots, then sauté them, remove and set aside. Toss the mushrooms in the lemon juice in a bowl, then sauté them in 15g/½oz of the butter. Remove and set aside.

Prepare the croutons by cutting each slice of bread in half to make triangles. Chop the remaining garlic clove in half and rub over the bread. Cook in the remaining butter in the frying pan until golden on both sides and crisp. Drain on paper towels and set aside.

When the beef is cooked, transfer it to a plate. Strain the rest of the contents of the casserole through a large fine sieve into a saucepan. Return the beef to the casserole, add the garnish of sautéed carrots, pickling onions and mushrooms, cover and set aside.

To make the sauce, discard the carrots and bouquet garni from the sieve. Remove the onions and garlic from the sieve and purée them. Add to the liquid in the pan and bring to the boil. Simmer, uncovered, for 30 minutes, skimming off any fat. Season to taste. Add the sauce to the casserole and gently heat through for 15-20 minutes, skimming off any further fat. Serve from the casserole with the parsley and croutons scattered over the top.

POT AU FEU DE SAINT-CHRISTOPHE AVEC UNE SAUCE VERTE

Boiled Burgundy Beef with a Green Herb Sauce

Also called bouilli, *this is usually eaten on the Thursday morning after the cattle market of Saint-Christophe-en-Brionnais. Assumption day (August 15th) is celebrated in Saint-Christophe by the cooking of a giant bouilli. Served with a green herb sauce, this makes a dish worthy of any feast.*

SERVES 4-6
800g/1¾lb of silverside, rib or chuck steak
4 pork sausages
4 slices trimmed thick back bacon, coarsely chopped
1 small marrow bone
3 leeks
4 small carrots
2 small turnips
1 celery stick
2 garlic cloves
1 onion studded with 2 cloves
1 bouquet garni
550g/1¼lb potatoes, peeled
1tbsp tapioca (optional)
pinch of salt

FOR THE GREEN SAUCE
3 anchovy fillets
1 large bunch of fresh flat-leaf parsley, finely chopped
4 gherkins, finely chopped
1tbsp capers, drained and finely chopped
½ garlic clove, finely chopped
2tbsp white wine vinegar
6tbsp olive oil
salt and freshly ground black pepper

Put all the vegetables, garlic, clove-studded onion, bouquet garni and salt in a very large saucepan or flame-proof casserole. Add 2l/1¾pt of water and bring to the boil. When the water is boiling, add the meat and marrow bone and simmer over a low heat for 1 hour and 10 minutes. Skim off any fat or scum.

Meanwhile, prepare the green sauce. Finely chop the anchovies and pound to a paste in a mortar with a pestle. Transfer the paste to a bowl and stir in the parsley, gherkins, capers, garlic and vinegar. Whisk in the olive oil a little at a time to make a thick sauce. Season to taste. Leave to stand for 30 minutes.

When the meat is ready, add the potatoes and cook for a further 10 minutes or until they are tender. Drain the meat and vegetables and reserve the broth. You can add 1 tablespoon of tapioca to thicken the broth, if you prefer.

Serve the meat surrounded by the vegetables with sea salt, gherkins and mustard. Serve the green sauce and the broth in separate bowls.

GATEAU BRESSAN

Cheese Tart

This is perfect for a Sunday morning breakfast or brunch. It is found in bakeries throughout southern Burgundy, and is often called cion *or* tapinette.

SERVES 4
200ml/8fl oz fromage frais
1tbsp plain flour
150ml/5fl oz single cream
85g/3oz sugar
2 eggs, separated
finely grated zest of 1 lemon
juice of 1 lemon (optional)
30g/1oz butter, diced

FOR THE DOUGH
250g/8½oz plain flour
5.5g/1½tsp dried yeast
30g/1oz sugar
100ml/3½fl oz milk
30g/1oz butter, softened
1tsp salt
1 egg, lightly beaten
3tbsp marc or brandy

Make sure that all the dough ingredients are at room temperature. To make the dough, sift the flour into a bowl. Make a well in the centre and add the yeast, 1tbsp sugar and 2tbsp of the milk. Cover and leave in a warm place for about 15 minutes until the yeast in the well froths. Add the remaining ingredients to the well, gradually drawing in the flour to make a smooth dough.

Knead the dough for 5 minutes by hand or machine until it is smooth and elastic. Leave the dough to rise for 1 hour, covered, in a warm place, until doubled in size.

Roll out the dough until it is 6mm/¼in thick and transfer it to a buttered 27cm/10¾in tart tin with a removable base. Leave in a warm place for about 15 minutes until the dough has risen slightly.

Meanwhile, preheat the oven to 220°C/425°F/gas mark 7. In a mixing bowl, beat the fromage frais with the flour, cream, 55g/2oz of the sugar, the egg yolks, lemon zest and lemon juice to taste. Beat the egg whites and fold them into the mixture. Spread over the risen dough, leaving a small space all around the edge. Dot with the diced butter.

Bake for 30 minutes, covering with foil if the filling becomes too brown.

Sprinkle with the remaining sugar and bake for 5 minutes more. Serve hot or leave to cool, removing the base of the tin before serving.

CREME A LA FEUILLE DE PECHER

White Cream Pudding Scented with Peach Leaves

If you do not have access to a peach tree, you can use ground almonds or a vanilla pod to flavour the milk. Use 150g/5½oz ground almonds or 1 vanilla pod for 250ml/8fl oz milk.

SERVES 4
250ml/8fl oz milk
3tbsp sugar
6 peach leaves
1 sachet powered gelatine
250ml/8fl oz single cream
1 peach or pear, peeled and cut into bite-size pieces
fresh strawberries and mint leaves, to decorate

FOR THE FRUIT COULIS
300g/10½oz raspberries and redcurrants, or apricots
2-4 tbsp sugar

Place the milk, the sugar and the peach leaves in a saucepan and warm gently, stirring well until the sugar has dissolved. Remove from the heat and leave to stand for 30 minutes.

Place a heat-proof bowl over a saucepan of steaming water and add 3 tablespoons of hot water to the bowl. Sprinkle the gelatine over the water and stir briskly until thoroughly mixed. Remove from the heat and let cool.

Take the peach leaves or vanilla pod out of the milk. Stir the cooled gelatine into the milk, taking care that there are no lumps. Mix in the cream, the peach or pear pieces and pour the mixture into a 575ml/1pt ring mould. Chill the pudding for 3 hours, or until it has set.

For the coulis, press the fruit through a sieve into a saucepan. Add the sugar and cook for 5 minutes or until the sugar has dissolved. Allow to cool.

Just before serving, let the ring mould stand in hot water for a few seconds. Unmould on to a large plate, surround with the coulis and decorate with mint leaves and strawberries.

CREPES AUX GAUDES AVEC COMPOTE DE PRUNES

Cornmeal Pancakes with Plum Compôte
(Illustrated opposite)

FOR 20 PANCAKES
45g/1½oz grilled cornmeal
85g/3oz plain flour

2 eggs
1tbsp vegetable oil
½ tsp salt
1tbsp kirsch
500ml/16fl oz milk
vegetable oil for frying

FOR THE PLUM COMPOTE
700g/1 ⅔ lb small plums, halved and stoned
1 cinnamon stick
150g/5 ½ oz sugar

Place the plums and the cinnamon stick in a large saucepan, cover with the sugar and leave to stand for 30 minutes to 1 hour, depending on the ripeness of the plums, to soften the plums and extract the juices. Place the saucepan over a gentle heat, cover and cook for about 10 minutes, stirring occasionally, until the plums have softened. Remove from the heat and leave to cool.

To make the pancakes, sift the cornmeal and plain flour into a bowl and make a well in the centre. Add the eggs, oil, salt, kirsch and 150ml/5fl oz of the milk to the well and whisk, slowly incorporating the flour from the edges. Whisk in the rest of the milk little by little, combining it gradually with the flour to make a smooth batter. Leave to stand for 2-3 hours.

Preheat the oven to 110°C/225°F/gas mark ¼.

Heat a small frying pan over a high heat, then grease it with a teaspoon of oil. Turn down the heat to medium and add about 2 tablespoons of batter. Tip the pan to spread the batter evenly. After about 30 seconds lift up the edge of the pancake with a palette knife. When it is lightly brown underneath, turn it over and brown the other side. Keep the pancakes warm in a covered oven-proof dish in the oven. Put a dessertspoon of plum compôte in the centre of each pancake then fold into quarters. Serve with fromage frais.

CORNIOTTES BOURGUIGNONNES

Triangular-shaped Pastries Filled with Fresh Fruit

In the town of Louhans, corniottes are filled with choux pastry, to make a rather unusual combination. Traditionally they are filled with cream cheese. In this recipe, however, they are filled with seasonal fruits. (Illustrated right)

MAKES 8
675g/1½ lb blackberries, blueberries, redcurrants or plums, or a mixture
5-6tbsp sugar
1 egg, beaten lightly with ½ tsp salt
150ml/4fl oz whipping cream
2tbsp icing sugar

FOR THE PASTRY
200g/7oz plain flour
100g/3½ oz unsalted butter, softened and diced
1tbsp sugar
½ tsp salt
1 egg yolk, lightly beaten

To make the pastry, sift the flour into a mixing bowl and make a large well in the centre. Using your fingertips quickly work the butter, sugar, salt, egg yolk and 2 tablespoons of cold water into the flour until well absorbed. Cover the bowl with cling film and chill for at least 30 minutes. Line a baking tray with greaseproof paper and set aside.

Roll out the pastry until it is about 6mm/½ in thick and cut eight rounds measuring 12.5cm/5in in diameter each. Mix the chosen fruit with the sugar and place a tablespoonful in the centre of each round.

Brush the edges of the dough with some of the beaten egg and fold them in from 3 directions to form a triangular shaped parcel that neatly encloses the fruit. Pinch the edges of the parcel to seal, and turn them up. Place on the baking tray and chill for 30 minutes.

Meanwhile, preheat the oven to 190°C/375°F/gas mark 4.

Brush the pastries with the remaining egg to glaze and bake for 20-25 minutes until they are golden.

Whip the cream with the icing sugar until it forms soft peaks. Serve the *corniottes* with the whipped cream.

TARTES AUX CASSIS

Blackcurrant and Almond Tarts

This recipe was given to me by Madame Lespinasse, my landlady in the Mâconnais. The tartness of the blackcurrant contrasts wonderfully with the sweetness of the pastry. (Illustrated opposite)

MAKES 4 SMALL TARTS
2 eggs
100g/3½ oz sugar
100g/3½ oz ground almonds
85g/3oz butter, melted, plus extra for greasing
½ tsp vanilla or almond essence
250g/8½ oz blackcurrants, fresh, frozen or tinned
30g/1oz flaked almonds

FOR THE PASTRY
250g/8½ oz plain flour
125g/4½ oz icing sugar
4 egg yolks
pinch of salt
150g/5½ oz butter, softened and diced
½ tsp vanilla or almond essence

TO DECORATE
100g/3½ oz apricot jam, melted (optional)
a few sprigs blackcurrant or leaves of almond paste (optional)

To make the pastry, sift the flour and icing sugar into a bowl. Make a well in the centre. Add the egg yolks, salt, butter and essence and mix with a fork until all the flour is absorbed. Wrap in cling film and chill for 1 hour.

Prepare the filling by beating the eggs with the sugar until the mixture is frothy, then beat in the almonds, butter and the essence.

Defrost the blackcurrant if frozen, or drain if tinned. Preheat the oven to 190°C/375°F/gas mark 6. Butter four 10cm/4in tart tins.

Roll out the pastry into 4 circles large enough to line each tart tin. Lift the dough with the rolling pin and press it into the tins, trimming off the edges. Distribute the blackcurrants over the bottom of the tarts, cover with the almond filling and sprinkle with the flaked almonds. Bake for 35 minutes until browned. Leave to cool on a wire rack. Brush the jam over the tarts to make a glaze and decorate with the blackcurrant sprigs or almond paste leaves.

A VISITOR'S GUIDE

The restaurants chosen in this guide cover a vast range of different cuisine and prices, but all offer Burgundian specialities. Lunchtime menus are often very good value even in the more expensive establishments but the choice of dishes is inevitably smaller. Some of the establishments I have indicated with three symbols are among the best restaurants in France and in the world so, though expensive, are certainly worth a stop (see below for key to indicate price ranges).

Fermes-auberges are a special type of restaurant, run by a working farm owner and usually offering food produced on the farm or on neighbouring farms and serving only Burgundian wines and spirits. Generous portions of home-cooking are offered; most places are only open at weekends, except during the summer months of July and August. For these reasons, it is often advisable to book ahead and even to order your meal in advance.

It is worth telephoning most places before visiting to enquire about opening times. Most towns have a Syndicat d'Initiative or a Mayor's office which will provide information for the various fairs and festivals listed here. Several towns have large tourist information offices.

It is advisable to call vineyards before making a visit. This should not be necessary for wine shops and the Maison des Vins. For more information on visiting vineyards, and on wines,

wine seminars and wine-tasting, contact the Bureau Interprofessionel des Vins de Bourgogne (BIVB) in Beaune, Mâcon and Chablis, and the Tourist Office in Beaune.

Most towns have celebrations for the festival of Saint-Jean in June and for Bastille day on July 14th.

Key to symbols used in this Guide:
••• expensive restaurants
•• middle-range restaurants
• inexpensive, simple restaurants

L'YONNE

Restaurants

A LA COTE SAINT-JACQUES •••
14 fg Paris, 89300 Joigny
Tel 86 62 09 70

BARNABET ••
14 quai de la République
89000 Auxerre, tel 86 51 68 88

LA CHAMAILLE ••
89240 Chavannes
Tel 86 41 24 80

GRANDE CHAUMIERE ••
3 rue Capucins, 89600 Saint-Florentin
Tel 86 35 15 12

HOSTELLERIE DES CLOS ••
18 rue Jules Rathier, 89800 Chablis
Tel 86 42 10 63

LA LUCARNE AUX CHOUETTES •
quai Bretoche
89500 Villeneuve-sur-Yonne
Tel 86 87 18 26

AUBERGE LES TILLEULS •
8990 Vincelottes
Tel 86 42 22 13

L'ESPERANCE •••
89450 Saint-Père-sous-Vézelay
Tel 86 33 20 45 (see pages 28-9)

LE LION D'OR •
rue L. Cormier
Toucy
Tel 86 44 00 76

LE CHEVAL BLANC •
4 rue des Ponts, Charny
Tel 86 63 60 66

LE POT D'ETAIN •
89440 L'Isle sur Serein
Tel 86 33 88 10

ABBAYE SAINT MICHEL ••
rue Saint-Michel
89700 Tonnerre
Tel 86 75 72 92

FERME-AUBERGE
"LES PERRIAUX" •
89520 Champignolles
Tel 86 45 13 22

Places of interest

MAISON DE LA VIGNE ET DU VIN
(information on wines)
28 rue Auxerroise
89800 Chablis
Tel 86 42 42 22

LA FERME DU CHATEAU
(turn-of-the-century working farm;
sale of produce on Sunday afternoons)
89170 Saint-Fargeau
Tel 86 74 03 76

MALLET FILS
(pottery)
route de Cosne
58310 Saint-Amand-en-Puisaye
Tel 86 39 60 80

ECOLE DE CUISINE
"LA VARENNE"
(classical cooking school)
Château du Fëy
Villecien
89300 Joigny
Tel 86 63 18 34

Specialities of the region

SEGMA LIEBIG MAILLE
(gherkins of Appoigny)
c/o 12 boulevard Eiffel, 21000 Dijon
Tel 80 63 02 30

JEAN MOREAU
(venison)
route d'Ormoy, 89210 Brienon
Tel 86 56 14 23

ROUSSELET
(*andouillette*)
15 rue Auxerroise, 89800 Chablis
Tel 86 42 11 28

ROY
(duck foie gras, sausages, smoked or
dried *magrets*, prepared dishes)
Le Paysan Bourguignon
Les Drillons, Beugnon
89600 Saint-Florentin
Tel 86 35 35 50

MARIANNE FOUCHET
(organic market garden)
rue des Ecoles
89450 Vézelay
Tel 86 33 31 66

SYNDICAT DES PRODUCTEURS DE
TRUFFE DE L'YONNE
Chambre d'Agriculture de l'Yonne
14 bis rue Guynemer
89015 Auxerre
Tel 86 46 47 48

MICHEL JALADE
(truffles)
6 rue de Quincy, 89430 Commissey
Tel 86 75 75 23

FRANCIS MARQUET
(asparagus of Vergigny)
1 rue du Puits
89600 Saint-Floretin
Tel 86 35 33 68

GOULLEY
(*coco de cheu*)
40 rue du Bois, 89600 Cheu
Tel 86 43 42 11

JEAN-YVES LEMOULE
(cherries, wine, ratafia)
Coulanges-la-Vineuse
Tel 86 42 37 32

PATRICK BARBOTIN
(hazelnuts, prunes, cherries)
7 rue Neuve, 89290 Jussy
Tel 86 53 38 20

M. LEBOULANGER
(*gougères*)
51 rue de l'Hôpital, 89700 Tonnerre
Tel 86 55 02 05

GERARD LECLERE
(Soumaintrain cheese)
La Jonctière
89570 Soumaintrain
Tel 86 56 31 06

FROMAGERIE LINCET
(regional cheeses)
89100 Saligny
Tel 86 97 83 97

BOULANGERIE PLANCHET
(*croquets*)
Grand-Rue
89520 Saint-Sauveur-en-Puisaye
Tel 86 45 55 17

*ABOVE The hill town of Vézelay.
To the left is the tower of the
Basilique Sainte Madeleine, once
an important pilgrimage site. It was
here that the supposed relics of
Mary Magdelene were housed.
However, the papal declaration of
1295 that they were not the
Magdelene's relics meant that its
significance declined.*

*RIGHT An intriguing doorway in
Saint-Florentin.
ABOVE The statue of Saint Nicolas,
patron saint of the sailors
of Auxerre, erected in 1714 by the
Confraternity of Saint Nicolas.*

*TOP A vineyard near Chablis. The northern location of these vineyards means that they are frequently subject to frosts from the end of March to the middle of May.
ABOVE The Renaissance chateau of Ancy-le-France. The chateau is set in magnificent grounds which include a lake and an island folly.*

LES DELOMAS
(honey)
Apidelis, 89120 Perreux
Tel 86 91 63 41

GIE LES OUCHES
(*raisiné* - grape conserve)
ferme de Miséry, 89480 Crain
Tel 86 81 74 27

ETS DOISNON
(honey, meringues, *pain d'épices*)
6 route de Paris
89300 Saint-Aubin-sur-Yonne
Tel 86 62 43 01

PHILLIPE CHARLOIS
(cider and ratafia)
Le Champion, 89770 Boeurs-en-Othe
Tel 86 88 00 29

JEAN-MARIE GOIS
(organic cider and apple juice)
Clos de Rochy, 89120 Dicy
Tel 86 63 67 03

Markets

Monday: *Saint-Florentin, Sens*
Tuesday: *Auxerre, Villeneuve-sur-Yonne*
Wednesday: *Joigny*
Friday: *Auxerre, Sens, Villeneuve-sur-Yonne*
Saturday: *Auxerre, Joigny, Saint-Florentin*

Fêtes

January 31st: *horse fair*, Saint-Sauveur-en-Puisaye
January, February: *Festival of Saint Vincent Tournante*, (*wine festival*), Chablis
June (last weekend) or July (first weekend): *cherry festival*, Escolives-Sainte-Camille
August: *harvest festival*, Etigny
2nd Saturday in September: *Melon and onion fair*, Joigny
4th Sunday in November: *Wine Festival*, Chablis
December 6th: *Foire aux Bovins (food fair)*, Saint-Sauveur-en-Puisaye

Vineyards

DELEGATION REGIONALE BUREAU
Interprofessionel des Vins de Bourgogne (BIVB)
(Chablis)
Le Petit Pontigny, 89800 Chablis
Tel 86 42 42 22

CAVE LA CHABLISIENNE
(Chablis)
8 bd Pasteur, 89800 Chablis
Tel 86 42 89 00

BERNARD LEGLAND
(Chablis premier Cru)
Domaine des Marroniers
89800 Préhy
Tel 86 41 42 70

DOMAINE CHAMPEIX-FOURNILLON
(Chablis)
Epineuil, 89360 Bernouil
Tel 86 55 50 96

ANITA AND JEAN-PIERRE COLINOT
(Bourgogne Irancy)
1 rue des Chariats
89290 Irancy
Tel 86 42 33 25

DOMAINE SORIN DEFRANCE
(Sauvignon de Saint-Bris)
11 bis rue de Paris
98530 Saint-Bris-la-Vineux
Tel 86 53 32 99

ROGER DELALOGE
(Bourgogne Irancy)
1 ruelle du Milieu
89290 Irancy
Tel 86 42 20 94

SYLVAIN MOSNIER
(Chablis Vieilles Vignes)
Beines, 89800 Chablis, tel 86 42 43 96

JEAN-PIERRE MALTOFF
(Coulanges-la-Vineuse)
20 rue d'Aguesseau
89580 Coulanges-la-Vineuse
Tel 86 42 24 92

LA VEZELIENNE
(Bourgogne Chardonnay)
route de Nanchèvre
89450 Saint-Père-sous-Vézelay
Tel 86 33 29 62

SICA DU VIGNOBLE AUXERROIS
(Crémant de Bourgogne)
Caves de Bailly, 89530 Bailly
Tel 86 53 34 00

RENE AND VINCENT DAUVISSAT
(Chablis)
8 rue Emile Zola, 89800 Chablis
Tel 86 42 11 58

DOMAINE GOUNOT (Petit Chablis)
Porte de Cravant
89800 Saint-Cyr-les-Colons
Tel 86 41 41 67

JEAN-CLAUDE COURTAULT (Chablis)
4 rue du Moulin, 89800 Maligny
Tel 86 47 44 76

GERARD ROBIN (Chablis)
3 rue Emile Zola, 89800 Chablis
Tel 86 42 18 19

SYLVAIN MOSNIER (Chablis)
4 rue Derrière-les-Murs, 89800 Beines
Tel 86 42 10 26

LE MORVAN

ABOVE *A cobbled street in Avallon showing a range of architectural styles. The Tour de l'Horloge and the building to the right were built in the mid-fifteenth century.* LEFT *Café-goers enjoy the late autumn sunshine in Autun.*

Restaurants

L'AUBERGE DE L'ATRE ••
(see pages 52-3)
Quarré-Les-Tombes
89630 Les Lavaults, tel 86 32 20 79

LA COTE D'OR ••• (see pages 50-1)
2 rue d'Argentine, 21210 Saulieu
Tel 80 64 07 66

HOTEL DE LA POSTE
1 rue Grillot, 21210 Saulieu
Tel 80 64 10 82

HOTEL LES URSULINES ••
14 rue Rivault, 71400 Autun
Tel 85 52 68 00

LE CHALET BLEU •
3 rue Jeannin, 71400 Autun
Tel 85 86 27 30

RICHARD AND M.-CHRISTINE
ORTYNSKI •
Ferme Auberge "Les Chaumes
de Ligny"
58330 Saint-Benin-des-Bois
Tel 86 58 20 48

BIBBI LEE AND CHARLIE SIMONDS •
Château de Lesvault, Onlay
58370 Villapourçon, tel 86 84 32 91

Places of interest

MOULIN DE MAUPERTUIS
(old mill and eco-museum)
Donzy, tel 86 39 39 46

MUSEE DU SEPTENNAT
(presidential museum)
6 rue du Château
58120 Château-Chinon
Tel 86 57 80 90

MAISON DU PARC NATUREL
REGIONAL DU MORVAN
(information and exhibitions on
the Morvan Park)
58230 Saint-Brisson
Tel 86 78 70 16

Specialities of the region

BOULANGERIE DECHAUME
44 rue du Marche, 21210 Saulieu
Tel 80 64 18 72

M. ET MME. DUVIGNAUD
(*gougères*)
Patisserie Guillemand, 11 rue Marche
21210 Saulieu, tel: 80 64 17 13

PATISSERIE LA FONTAINE
24 place de l'Eglise
89630 Quarré-les-Tombes
Tel 86 32 22 21

TOP *The landscape near Onlay. As in much of the Morvan, the fields are divided by hedges.* ABOVE *In many parts of rural Burgundy, cafés serve many functions. This one, near Liernais, is a restaurant, the local shop, and a bakery.* RIGHT *A kid sheltering from the sun.*

DOMINIQUE LEHUJEUR (pigeons)
Athée, 58140 Saint-André-en-Morvan
Tel 86 22 66 01

PIERRE AND MARIE-ALICE
DELOMEZ GIE
Les Colombiers de Puisaye
et du Morvan (pigeons, terrines)
58310 Bouhy, tel 86 26 44 15

MICHELINE GAUDRY
(Morvan ham, *andouilles*, *saucisson*)
25 place Saint-Romain
58120 Château-Chinon, tel 86 85 13 87

M. MARACHE (trout, smoked fish)
La Serrée, Alligny-en-Morvan
Tel 86 76 15 79

GERARD MATERNAUD
(fruit, vegetables, mushrooms)
Les Guichards
89630 Quarré-les-Tombes
Tel 86 32 20 94

LUC DIGONNET
Fromagerie de Siloé (goats' cheese)
Changy, Le Mousseau
58370 Villapourçon, tel 86 78 63 43

M. GUYONNET (ewe's milk cheese)
Thard, 58370 Onlay
Tel 86 84 24 57

ABBAYE DE LA PIERRE-QUI-VIRE
(fresh cheese)
89830 Saint-Léger-Vauban
Tel 86 32 21 23

ALBERT MARTIN (buckwheat flour)
Moulin-de-la-Presle
Planchez, tel 86 78 43 46

JEAN-JACQUES AND DOMINIQUE
COPPIN
Les Ruchers du Morvan
(wild honey, *pain d'épices*, beeswax)
Port de l'Homme
Corancy, 58120 Château-Chinon
Tel 86 78 02 43

BERNARD BERILLEY
(jams)
La Trinqlinette, Trinquelin
89630 Quarré-les-Tombes
Tel 86 32 20 97

JACQUES SULEM
(jams and jam-making lessons)
Poiseux, Saint-Léger-de-Fougeret
Tel 86 85 10 44

M. COMELOUP, MAYOR
Syndicat des Producteurs de
Marrons du Morvan
(chestnuts)
Saint-Léger-sous-Beuvray
Tel 85 82 53 00

Markets

Tuesday: Quarré-les-Tombes
Thursday: Avallon
Friday: Autun
Saturday: Avallon, Saulieu

Fêtes

May: *Journées Gourmandes du Grand Morvan*, (gastronomic festival), Saulieu
August: *Fête du Charolais*, (cattle show), Saulieu; *Blueberry Fair*, Glux-en-Glenne
October: *Chestnut Fair*, Saint-Léger-sous Beuvray

LA COTE D'OR

Restaurants

JEAN-PAUL THIBERT ••
10 place Wilson, 21000 Dijon
Tel 80 67 74 64

JEAN-PIERRE BILLOUX ••
14 place Darcy, 21000 Dijon
Tel 80 30 11 00

HOST. CHAPEAU ROUGE ••
5 rue Michelet, 21000 Dijon
Tel 80 30 28 10

BISTRO LE DOME •
rue Quentin, 21000 Dijon
Tel 80 30 58 92

LE VIEUX MOULIN ••
21420 Bouilland, tel 80 21 51 16

CHEZ CAMILLE ••
1 place Edouard-Herriot,
21230 Arnay-le-Duc, tel 80 90 01 38

LA CIBOULETTE •
69 rue de Lorraine, 21200 Beaune
Tel 80 24 70 72

L'ECUSSON •
place Malmédy, 21200 Beaune
Tel 80 24 03 82

LE JARDIN DES RAMPARTS ••
10 rue Hôtel-Dieu, 21200 Beaune
Tel 80 24 79 41

JEAN CROTET ••
route de Combertault, 21200 Levernois
Tel 80 24 73 58

LA BOUZEROTTE •
21200 Bouze-les-Beaune
Tel 80 26 01 37

LE RESTAURANT DES MINIMES •
39 rue de Vaux
23140 Sémur-en-Auxois
Tel 80 97 26 86

L'ARMANCON ••
Chailly-sur-Armançon
Tel 85 33 33 99

LE VAL DES MAS •
M. et Mme. Mouillefarine
21510 Beaunotte
Tel 80 93 81 43

Places of Interest

WINE PRESSES OF THE DUKES
OF BURGUNDY (the oldest and
largest wine presses in Burgundy)
Chenove, tel 80 52 51 30

MAISON REGIONALES DES ARTS DE
LA TABLE
(history of food and food utensils)
Anciens Hospices Saint-Pierre
15 rue Saint Jacques, Arnay-le-Duc
Tel 80 90 11 59

MUSEE DU VIN DE BOURGOGNE
(history of wine in Burgundy)
rue d'Enfer, 21200 Beaune

MAISON DES CONFRERIES
(history of confraternities)
20 rue du Faubourg Madeleine
Beaune, tel 80 24 05 05

MUSEE DE LA VIE
BOURGUIGNONNE
Perrin de Puycousin
(scenes from shops and workshops of
the nineteenth century)
17 rue Saint-Anne, 21000 Dijon
Tel 80 30 65 91

MUSEE DES ARTS ET DES
TRADITIONS DES HAUTES-COTES
(history of the region's vineyards)
21700 Reulle-Vergy, tel 80 61 12 54

*ABOVE One of Marlet's sculpted lions
decorates a staircase leading to
the ramparts of Beaune.
LEFT A market stall in Dijon displays
an array of tempting produce.*

MAISON DU SEIGLE
(eco-museum)
Menessaire
Tel 80 64 28 65

AMORA MUSTARD MUSEUM
(telephone for an appointment)
21000 Dijon, tel 80 30 35 39

CIRCUITS GOURMANDS: day visits
are now available which go to five
locations: the Hautes Côtes, l'Auxois,
Mont-Saint-Jean, Salives and the
Chatillonais. These include a lunch in
a typical restaurant and visits to local
farms and producers. Details can be
obtained from:
Tourist Office of Côte d'Or,
Hôtel du Département, 21000 Dijon
Tel 80 63 66 00

Specialities of the region

SYLVAIN MANSUY (snails)
élèvage Marsannay le Bois
Tel 80 35 76 15/80 71 69 63

L'ESCARGOT (fresh snails)
14 rue Bannelier
21000 Dijon
Tel 80 30 22 15

REMY GARROT
(pleurote mushrooms)
21540 Sombernon
Tel 80 33 45 20

EDMOND FALLOT (mustard)
31 Faubourg Bretonniere
21200 Beaune
Tel 80 22 10 02

MME. SIGOILLOT
(free-range chickens, ducks,
guinea fowl, fresh cream)
21510 Duesme, Aignay-le-Duc
Tel 80 93 87 89

CHANTAL AND DANIEL BORGEOT
(jambon persillé, hams and
saucissons)
21590 Santenay-les-Bains
Tel 80 20 61 71

PATRICK GEVREY (charcutier)
11 rue Jean-Jacques-Rousseau
21000 Dijon, tel 80 07 39 38

RAYMOND FIQUET
(tripes and boudins)
Halles Centrales
Dijon 21000
Tel 80 30 79 05

HERVE AND ODILE PINCZON
DU SEL (Epoisses cheeses)
Ferme du Colombier
Sivry, 21230 Arnay-le-Duc
Tel 80 90 03 07

FROMAGERIE PORCHERET
(cheeses)
18 rue Bannelier, Dijon 21000
Tel 80 30 21 05

ABBAYE DE CITEAUX (cheese)
21000 Saint-Nicholas-les-Citeaux
Tel 80 61 11 53

FROMAGERIES BERTHAULT
(cheeses)
place du Champs-de-Foire
21460 Epoisses
Tel 80 96 44 44

PATISSERIE GOURMANDINE
18 rue Monge, 21200 Beaune
Tel 80 22 24 03

MULOT ET PETITJEAN
(*pain d'épices*)
16 rue de la Liberté, 21000 Dijon
Tel 80 30 07 10

GAUTHIER
(regional products and wines)
77 rue Jean-Jacques-Rousseau, 21000
Dijon, tel 80 67 17 19

GERARD GUILLEMINOT (vegetables)
route de Varois
21490 Ruffey-Les-Echirey
Tel 80 36 07 43

OLIVIER
(homemade liqueurs and jams)
Concoeur-et-Corboin
21700 Nuits-Saint-Georges
Tel 80 61 00 43

GILLES JOANNET
(fruit liqueurs and crèmes)
rue Basse, Arcenant
21700 Nuits-Saint-Georges
Tel 80 61 12 23

TROUBAT
(Anis de l'Abbaye de Flavigny)
Abbaye de Flavigny
21150 Flavigny-sur-Ozerain
Tel 80 96 20 88

Markets

Daily: *Dijon*, around the central *halles*
(plus more stalls on Tuesdays and
Fridays)

Thursday: *Arnay-le-Duc*
Friday: *Montbard*
Saturday: *Châtillon-sur-Seine, Seurre, Saint-Jean-de-Losne*

Fêtes

end of January: *Festival of Saint Vincent Tournante* (the patron saint of wine), changes location every year
March or April: *Wine Sale of the Hospices*, Nuits-Saint-Georges
May: *Wine Fair*, Rouvray
May 31st: *Fête de la Bague* (traditional horse race), Sémur-en-Auxois
August: *Regional Fair*, Montbard
September: *Wine Rally*, Beaune; *Fête de la Vigne* (festival of wine) Dijon; *Fête du Roi Chambertin* (wine feast), Chambertin
October/November: *Foire Internationale Gastronomique* (international food fair), Dijon
November (third weekend): wine festival of *Les Trois Glorieuses*, held throughout the region over three days (see page 65). Saturday evening: *Chapter meeting of the Confrérie des Chevaliers du Tastevin*, Clos de Vougeot; Sunday: *Wine Auction of the Wines of the Hospices de Beaune*, Beaune; Monday: *Paulée* (literary lunch), Meursault

Vineyards

MARIE-ANDREE AND CHANTAL GERBET
(Hautes Cotes de Nuits, Vosne-Romanée)
21700 Vosne-Romanée
Tel 80 61 07 85

DOMAINE PRIEURE-ROCH
(Henri Roch)
Vosne-Romanée
21700 Nuits-Saint-Georges
Tel 80 62 38 79

BIVB
12 boulevard de la Bretonniere
21204 Beaune, tel 80 24 70 20

DOMAINE GUY ROULOT (Meursault)
1 rue Charles Giraud
21190 Meursault, tel 80 21 21 65

DOMAINE MARC MOREY ET FILS
(Chassagne-Montrachet)
3 rue Charles Paquelin
21190 Chassagne-Montrachet
Tel 80 21 30 11

LUCIEN MUZARD (Santenay)
rue de la cour Verreuil
21590 Santenay, tel 80 20 61 85

DOMAINE RATEAU (Beaune)
Jean-Claude and Pierrette Rateau
chemin des Mariages, 21200 Beaune
Tel 80 22 52 54

GHISLAINE BARTHOD
(Chambolle-Musigny)
rue du Lavoir
21220 Chambolle Musigny
Tel 80 62 80 16

DOMAINE DE COURCEL (Pommard)
place de l'Eglise, 21630 Pommard
Tel 80 22 10 64

DOMAINE PIERRE GELIN (Fixin)
2 rue du Chapitre, 21220 Fixin
Tel 80 52 45 24

ALAIN MONTCHOVET
(Bourgogne Aligoté)
rue Rocault, 21190 Nantoux
Tel 80 26 03 13

CHRISTINE AND JEAN-MARC DURAND
(Bourgogne Hautes Côtes de Beaune)
1 rue des Vignes, 21200 Beaune
Tel 80 22 75 31

MAISON JOSEPH DROUHIN
7 rue d'Enfer, 21000 Beaune
Tel 80 24 68 88

DOMAINE PHILIPPE CHARLOPIN-PARIZOT
(Gevrey-Chambertin Vieilles Vignes)
18 route de Dijon
21220 Gevery-Chambertin
Tel 80 51 81 27

DOMAINE HENRI PERROT-MINOT
(Morey-Saint-Denis)
54 route des Grand-Crus
21220 Morey-Saint-Denis
Tel 80 34 32 51

L'HERITIER-GUYOT (Vougeot)
rue du Champ-aux-Prêtres
21100 Dijon, tel 80 72 16 14

DOMAINE DU CHATEAU DE PREMEAUX (Nuits-Saint-Georges)
21700 Premeaux-Prissey
Tel 80 62 30 64

DOMAINE MAILLARD PERE ET FILS
(Aloxe-Corton, Chorey-les-Beaune)
2 rue Joseph-Bard
21200 Chorey-les-Beaune
Tel 80 22 10 67

ABOVE The the thirteenth-century cellars of the negociant *Drouhin. OPPOSITE Harvesting near Gevrey-Chambertin. BELOW A wall painting depicting the grand cru wines of Gevrey. These are amongst the most prestigious wines in Burgundy.*

DOMAINE ROBERT ET RAYMOND
JACOB (Ladoix, Corton, Hautes Côtes
de Beaune)
Buisson, 21550 Ladoix-Serrigny
Tel 80 26 40 42

ROGER JAFFELIN ET FILS
(Pernand-Vergelesses)
21420 Pernand-Vergelesses
Tel 80 21 52 43

DOMAINE PIERRE GUILLEMOT
(Savigny-les-Beaune)
1 rue Boulanger-et-Vallée
21420 Savigny-les-Beaune
Tel 80 21 50 40

DOMAINE LOUIS VIOLLAND
(Beaune)
13 rue de l'Ancienne Poste
21200 Beaune, tel 80 22 24 86

PAUL GARAUDET
(Meursault, Monthélie)
imp. de l'Eglise, 21190 Monthélie
Tel 80 21 28 78

DOMAINE PASCAL PRUNIER
(Saint-Romain)
rue Traversière
21190 Auxey-Duresses
Tel 80 21 67 33

DOMAINE VINCENT GIRARDIN
(Santenay, Maranges)
route de Chassagne-Montrachet
21590 Santenay, tel 80 20 64 29

TONNELLERIE DAMY
21 rue des Forges
21190 Meursault
Tel 80 21 23 41

LA SAONE-ET-LOIRE

Restaurants

GREUZE •••
1 rue Thibaudet
71700 Tournus
Tel 85 51 13 52

LAMELOISE •••
36 place d'Armes
71150 Chagny
Tel 85 87 08 85

HOTELLERIE DU VAL D'OR ••
Grande-rue
71640 Mercurey
Tel 85 45 13 70

AUBERGE DU CEP ••
place de l'Eglise
Fleurie
Tel 74 04 10 77

MARITONNES ••
71570 Romaneche-Thorins
Tel 85 35 51 70

CHAPON FIN ET RESTAURANT PAUL
BLANC ••
01190 Thoissey, tel 74 04 04 74

LE RAISIN••
01190 Pont-de-Vaux
Tel 85 30 30 97

LEA ••
00190 Montrevel-en-Bresse
Tel 74 30 80 84

DENISE ET JEAN-NOEL
DAUVERGNE •
Restaurant de la Poste
71600 Poisson
Tel 85 81 10 72

PAUL GELIN
FERME AUBERGE DE LAVAUX •
Chatenay, 71800 La Clayette
Tel 85 28 08 48

LA FONTAINE •• (see pages 112-3)
71740 Châteauneuf
Tel 85 26 26 87

BOURGOGNE ••
place de l'Abbaye, 71250 Cluny
Tel 85 59 00 58

LA GARE •
avenue de la Gare, 71170 La Clayette
Tel 85 28 01 65

LE BISTROT •
31 rue de Strasbourg
71100 Chalon-sur-Saône
Tel 85 93 22 01

RIPERT •
31 rue Saint-Georges
71000 Chalon-sur-Saône
Tel 85 48 89 20

LE SAINT GEORGES •
32 avenue Jean-Jaurès,
71000 Chalon-sur-Saône
Tel 85 48 27 05

LE MOULIN DE BOURGCHATEAU •
chemin du Bourgchâteau
71500 Louhans
Tel 85 75 37 12

AUX TERRASSES •
18 avenue du 23 Janvier
71700 Tournus
Tel 85 51 01 74

FERME AUBERGE LES PLATTIERES •
71470 Sainte-Croix-en-Bresse
Tel 85 74 80 70

GEORGES BLANC •••
01540 Vonnas, tel 74 50 00 10

LE CHAROLAIS •
33 bis route Moulins, 58300 Decize
Tel 86 25 22 27

LE MANOIR DE SORNAT••
route de Moulins, Bourbon-Lancy
Tel 85 89 17 39

LES VIGNERONS ••
69840 Emeringes, tel 74 04 45 72

EDMOND RAVIDATI •
Ferme Auberge de Groboz
01350 Villemotier
Tel 74 30 17 79

Places of interest

ECO MUSEE DE LA BRESSE
BOURGUIGNONNE
(museum of rural traditions)
Chateau Saint Père
71270 Pierre de Bresse
Tel 85 76 27 16

MAISON DU BLE ET DU PAIN
(wheat and bread museum)
71350 Verdun-sur-le-Doubs
Tel 85 76 27 15

LA FERME DE SOUGEY
(typical Bressan working farm)
Montrevel-en-Bresse
Tel 74 25 47 12

LA FERME DE LA FORET
(seventeeth-century Bressan
farmhouse)
01560 Saint-Trivier des Courtes
Tel 74 30 71 89

MUSEE DU TERROIR AND POULTRY
(poultry museum)
71470 Romenay
Tel 85 40 30 90

Specialities of the region

JEANNINE AND GUY PUTIGNY
(vegetables and fruits)
120 rue Grandmort
71000 Epervans
Tel 85 96 02 99

M. GAUDRY
(Charolais butcher)
71800 Saint-Christophe-en-Brionnais
Tel 85 25 83 21

PHILLIPE AND HENRI VELUT
(Charolais cattle)
71800 Saint-Christophe-en-Brionnais
Tel 85 25 82 16

THIERRY AND CLAIRE JALLEY
(Bresse chicken)
71330 Sens-sur-Seille
Tel 85 74 76 23

S.A. MOUTON CHAROLAIS
(Charolais sheep)
36 rue Général Leclerc
71120 Charolles, tel 85 24 00 18

BERNARD JACQUES
(crayfish, freshwater fish)
71350 Verjux, tel 85 91 64 46

PAUL BUISSON (freshwater fish)
71260 Montbelay, tel 85 40 51 91

GILBERT MORESTIN
(frogs, freshwater fish)
71270 La Chapelle-Saint-Sauveur
Tel 85 36 75 08

MOULIN DE CHAUSSON (gaudes)
Michel Taron, 39120 Chausson
Tel 84 81 81 06

JEAN LEBLANC ET FILS (oil mill)
71340 Iguerand, tel 85 84 07 83

CHRISTIAN DONET
(goats' cheese, boutons de culotte)
71640 Saint-Denis-de-Vaux
Tel 85 44 44 91

LARUE (goats' cheese)
Grandvaux, 71120 Palinges
Tel 85 24 03 72

OPPOSITE LEFT The Ecomusée de la
Bresse Bourguignonne, housed in a
seventeenth-century chateau
at Pierre-de-Bresse.
OPPOSITE RIGHT The basilique du
Sacré Coeur at Paray-le-Monial.
TOP Two of the remaining
towers of the church of Cluny.
ABOVE A welcoming sign in Cluny.

ABOVE Christian Donet with one of his goats.
RIGHT Bresse chickens at the Jalley's farm at Sens-sur-Seille.
BELOW During the last century a pitcher of crème de cassis was to be found on each café table; customers would add it to their white wine to make a delicious aperitif.

OPPOSITE ABOVE Places such as this offer an opportunity to taste and learn about the wines of the region.
OPPOSITE BELOW A vigneron's house set among the vines of the Mâconnais.

PASCALE COTTIN & JEAN-LUC PERTILE
(goats' cheese)
Domaine de L'Argolay
71800 Saint-Germain-en-Brionnais
Tel 85 70 64 97

VINAUGER DUCHARNE
(fruit sirops, liqueurs)
Impasse Marmet
71800 La Clayette
Tel 85 28 01 41

GERBERON
(cacou, pastries)
14 rue des Deux Ponts
71600 Paray-le-Monial
Tel 85 81 45 89

BOUVIER
(cion, corniotte)
Aux Fiançailles
71500 Louhans
Tel 85 75 12 24

BERNARD DUFOUX
(chocolates and chocolate-making courses)
32 rue Centrale, 71800 La Clayette
Tel 85 28 08 10

CHATEAU DE L'AUBESPIN
(old-fashioned jams, fruits in honey and vinegar, aromatic vinegars)
71220 Saint-André-le-Desert
Tel 85 59 49 48

BERTRAND PERRAUDIN
(rye bread, brioche with pralines)
La Bruyère
71320 Charbonnat-sur-Arroux
Tel 85 54 28 24

MONTERRAT
Patisserie de La Barre
(cakes, chocolates)
39 rue de la Barre
71000 Mâcon
Tel 85 38 31 11

A. THEURET
Le Cygne de Montjeu
(patisserie)
12 rue Saint-Saulge
71400 Autun
Tel 85 52 29 61

Markets

Monday: *Louhans*
Thursday: *Saint-Christophe-en-Brionnais*
Friday: *Chalon-sur-Saône*
Saturday: *Bourbon-Lancy*, *Mâcon*
Sunday: *Chagny*

Fêtes

April (week of Mardi Gras): *Carnival*, Chalon-sur-Saône
May: Foire des Vins de France *(wine fair)*, Macon
mid-June to mid-July: *Festival du Beaujolais*, Villefranche-sur-Saône
end of July: *Horse Races*, La Clayette
August: Wine Fair, Chagny; (last weekend): *Foire de la Balme* (cattle market and fair), Bouhans, Saint-Germain-des-Bois
November: *Fernand Point Gastronomic Exhibition* (trainee cook competition), Louhans
December: *Turkey and Goose Fair*, Marcigny; *Bresse Chicken Fair*, Louhans

Vineyards

DELEGATION REGIONALE MACON
DU BIVB
389 avenue Mal-de-Lattre-de-Tassigny
71000 Mâcon
Tel 85 38 20 15

LA MAISON DES VINS DE LA COTE
CHALONNAISE
promenande Sainte-Marie
71100 Chalon-sur-Saône
Tel 85 41 64 00

LA MAISON MACONNAISE DES VINS
avenue Mal-de-Lattre-de-Tassigny
71000 Mâcon
Tel 85 38 62 51

RENE BOURGEON
(Givry)
Jambles
71640 Givry
Tel 85 44 35 85

DOMAINE JOBLOT
(Givry)
4 rue Pasteur
71640 Givry
Tel 85 44 30 77

MARCEL LAPIERRE
(Morgon)
69910 Villié-Morgon
Tel 74 04 23 89

ALAIN GERMAIN
(Chardonnay)
Domaine du Moulin Blanc
Crière
69380 Charnay
Tel 78 43 98 60

J.J. VINCENT
(Pouilly-Fuissé)
Château de Fuissé
71960 Fuissé
Tel 85 35 61 44

GEORGES DUBOEUF
La Gare, Romanèche-Thorins
Tel 85 35 51 13

CHATEAU DE CHENAS (Chénas)
69840 Chénas
Tel 74 04 48 19

C. COLLOVRAY AND J.L. TERRIER
(Saint-Véran)
Domaine des Deux-Roches
71960 Davayé
Tel 85 35 86 51

CAVE DE CHAINTRE
(Beaujolais supérieur)
71570 Chaintré
Tel 85 35 61 61

J.M. TRUCHOT
(Beaujolais)
GFA du Grand Talancé
69640 Denicé
Tel 74 67 55 04

RAYMOND MATHELIN ET FILS
(Chiroubles, Dom Melinand)
Domaine de Sandar
69380 Chatillon d'Azergues
Tel 78 43 92 41

DOMAINE JEAN MARECHAL
(Mercurey)
Grande Rue
71640 Mercurey
Tel 85 45 11 29

DOMAINE JEAN-CLAUDE BRELIERE
(Rully)
place de l'Eglise
71150 Rully
Tel 85 91 22 01

CAVE DE LUGNY
rue des Charmes
71260 Lugny
Tel 85 33 22 85

MOMMESSIN
(Fleurie)
La Grange Saint-Pierre
71850 Charnay-les-Mâcon
Tel 85 32 81 00

JEAN BUIRON
(Juliénas, Le Chapon)
69840 Juliénas
Tel 74 04 40 39

MAURICE AND CATHERINE GAY
(Moulin à Vent)
Les Vérillats
69840 Chénas
Tel 74 04 48 86

CAVE DES VIGNERONS DE BEL-AIR
(Régnié)
69220 Saint-Jean-d'Ardières
Tel 74 66 35 91

LORNON ET FILS
(Brouilly, Pontanevaux)
71570 La Chapelle de Guinchay
Tel 85 36 70 52

A. AND P. DE VILLAINE
(Bourgogne Côte Chalonnaise)
Au Bourg, 71150 Bouzeron
Tel 85 91 20 50

LIST OF RECIPES

INDEX

AUTHOR'S ACKNOWLEDGMENTS

'He reigned down manna also upon them for to eat and gave them food from heaven'. My most vivid memory of Burgundy is trawling through the countryside during the hot summer in a heavily-laden car looking like an immigrant going home, belongings piled high to the windows and on the roof - most of it belonged to the smallest member of the family, five-month-old Theodore. Winding our way through country lanes, arriving at a farmhouse or a vineyard, Hamish and I would take out the exhausted baby, place him on the grass with a bottle (of milk!), try wines and cheeses and participate for one moment in rural life, its joys and its hardships. It was exhilarating.

For all that and much more, I thank all the people of Burgundy who so kindly helped us, took us in, gave us their time and their knowledge with such enthusiasm and were unfailingly hospitable. Many are mentioned in this book; if I have omitted any, it is only due to lack of space.

I thank my parents, Alya and Saverio Callea who always encourage my curiosity and my thirst for knowledge and give without limits. Thank you to Natacha Hennocq for her support, the books, the au pair and answering my constant questions. Thank you to all those who helped with the recipes, who tested and tasted them, particularly my sister, Tamara Burnet-Smith, Jessica and Paul Staddon and Charlotte Coleman-Smith.

PHOTOGRAPHER'S ACKNOWLEDGMENTS

I have benefited from the generosity, assistance and hard work of numerous people. In Burgundy, Theresa Kelly, who looked after our five-month-old son, Theo, with great diligence; the Tilquins and Lespinasses, our landlords, who made us so welcome and the 'location team' of Karen, Meg, Cara and Ron, who overcame cold and inclement weather to produce the recipe shots. In London I should like to thank Lesley Stuart, Mary and John Wallace, Duncan Larraz, and the 'home team' Charlotte, Roisín, and Sarah Pearce. Finally, my thanks go to all those people in Burgundy whom we visited who taught us so much about the place and what they did; without them this book would not have been as rewarding.

PUBLISHER'S ACKNOWLEDGMENTS

For the recipe photography (pages 30, 32, 33, 35, 37, 54, 55, 57, 59, 60, 83, 84, 87, 88, 90, 92, 114, 116, 119, 121, 122, 125, 127)
Home Economist: Meg Jansz
Assistant: Cara Hobday
Stylist: Roisín Nield

Index: Karin Woodruff
Map (page 10):   Clare Melinsky
Recipe consultant: Anne Sheasby

The publisher would like to thank Liza Bruml, Jackie Matthews and Tessa Clayton for editorial work. The publisher also thanks Clare Blackwell, Alison Bolus, Jill Macey and Clive Smith.